The Joy
of Juicing

The Joy

Completely Revised & Updated

# of Juicing

Creative Cooking
with Your Juicer

Gary Null, Ph.D.

with Shelly Null

AVERY
a member of
Penguin Putnam Inc.
New York

Every effort has been made to ensure that the information contained in this book is complete and accurate. However, neither the publisher nor the author is engaged in rendering professional advice or services to the individual reader. The ideas, procedures, and suggestions contained in this book are not intended as a substitute for consulting with your physician. All matters regarding health require medical supervision. Neither the author nor the publisher shall be liable or responsible for any loss, injury, or damage allegedly arising from any information or suggestion in this book.

The recipes contained in this book are to be followed exactly as written. Neither the publisher nor the author is responsible for your specific health or allergy needs that may require medical supervision, or for any adverse reactions to the recipes contained in this book.

Most Avery books are available at special quantity discounts for bulk purchase for sales promotions, premiums, fund-raising, and educational needs. Special books or book excerpts also can be created to fit specific needs. For details, write Putnam Special Markets, 375 Hudson Street, New York, NY 10014.

AVERY

a member of Penguin Putnam Inc.
375 Hudson Street
New York, NY 10014
www.penguinputnam.com

Library of Congress Cataloging-in-Publication Data

Null, Gary.
    The joy of juicing : creative cooking with your juicer /
Gary Null, with Shelly Null.
        p.   cm.
    ISBN 1-58333-102-6
    1. Juicers.   2. Fruit juices.   3. Vegetable juices.
I. Null, Shelly.   II. Title.
TX840.J84 N85   2001   2001022360
641.8'75—dc21

Printed in the United States of America
10   9   8   7

This book is printed on acid-free paper. ♾

Front cover photograph of soup © Anthony Johnson/ImageBank
Book design by Tanya Maiboroda

Acknowledgments

I WOULD LIKE TO THANK Andre Turan and my entire New York staff for testing these recipes; Laura Shepherd, Carol Rosenberg, and Christopher Mariadason for their patience and editorial input; and finally the knowledgeable engineers who helped design my state-of-the-art home juicer.

Contents

Introduction   1

The Basics of Juicing   5

Juices and Shakes   7

Breakfast Foods   81

Soups   95

Salads   111

Dressings, Sauces, Dips, and Spreads   129

Main Dishes   149

Desserts   167

Gary Null's Natural-Living Weight-Loss Tips   213

Vegetarian's Vocabulary   217

Index   223

The Joy
of Juicing

Introduction to the New
Joy of Juicing Cookbook

IN THE SEVEN YEARS since the first edition of *The Joy of Juicing* was published, America's consciousness about the importance of altering the diet to maintain health has been substantially expanded. People have become increasingly aware of the importance of live (organic, unprocessed, whole) foods, and many Americans have become vegetarians. They now understand that these foods, with their available enzymes, antioxidants, and phytochemicals, can be the key to slowing down, and in many cases reversing, premature aging and a host of diseases such as heart disease, cancer, and arthritis. What's more, many people now go beyond taking a simple one-a-day vitamin; they're now taking additional supplements with an eye to specific concerns, such as vitamin E for the heart or vitamin C for immune function.

During these same seven years, I have conducted more than fifty health support groups reaching nearly 10,000 individuals. After an initial blood chemistry workup and medical evaluation, these people adopted lifestyle and dietary changes for a period of a year to a year and a half. At the end of that period, they were evaluated again, with dramatically improved results. (These success stories have been published in peer-reviewed journals, presented on PBS, and summarized in some of my books, such as *Gary Null's Ultimate Anti-Aging Program* and my *Ultimate Lifetime Diet*.)

These documented transformations provide a new model for wellness. In the past, if you had questions about what to eat, which vitamins to take, or how to exercise or handle stress, you went to your physician. Regrettably, physicians worked with a disease model, and thus were completely unprepared to provide information specific to optimizing health. Instead, patients walked away with a prescription for a drug or were told to go on doing everything they'd been doing, but in moderation. This allowed people to continue with the same habits that made them sick in the first place—consuming animal products and over-processed foods, containing harmful additives, such as excitotoxins; putting up with environmental pollution; and maintaining overly stressful lifestyles. It's no surprise then that this do-nothing approach actually did nothing to lessen the incidence of chronic disease. There are no "magic bullet" cures, and fad diets don't work for long either.

But we're in a new millennium now, and I have reason to be optimistic that America's attitude toward health is changing. The results from my health support groups are certainly encouraging. For the first time, a large number of people following a very specific protocol proved that individuals could slow down, and in some cases reverse disease by using a wellness model. In other words, these health support groups did not diagnose, treat, or address specific illness. Instead, we asked them to focus on what was needed to enhance their well-being. By changing their eating habits, increasing exercise, and managing stress better, the participants were able to affect tremendous improvement in their health and also set the stage for a whole new consciousness. I have been presenting this information across the country for the past three years. I've been gratified to help millions of other Americans expand their consciousness as well.

Here, in a nutshell, is my message: The cornerstone of the dietary approach to change is cleansing and detoxifying. The next step is healthier cells—actually repairing damaged DNA. While people are hoping for a miracle to repair disease, my research shows that you can repair cellular damage simply by using nature—if you access natural substances in the right quantities. Juicing and a live food diet are the heart of the program. Live food (note that this does not necessarily mean raw food) includes grains, legumes, vegetables, fruits, nuts, and seeds. And juicing is absolutely essential. Even if you improve your diet radically and take all the right supplements, while you'll be getting some measure of preventive benefit, you still won't be doing enough to reverse existing damage. Add juicing to the mix, though, and you can actually begin to repair damage. Juicing is the key to reversing the progress of disease.

The juicing component of my program is introduced gradually. Participants begin with one 12-ounce glass of fresh, organic juice a day, and stay at this level for the first month of the program. The second month they consume two glasses a day, and the amount is increased incrementally until at six months they consume six glasses a day. After one year, or a year and a half, the results, across the board, were impressive. All the individuals who sought weight loss achieved this goal—and this was without dieting in the traditional sense, and without counting calories. Some people lost over 150 pounds, and one individual lost 350. Secondly, long-term chronic illnesses, such as diabetes and arthritis, were dramatically improved or even eradicated. The same was true for people with fibromyalgia, fibrocystic breast disease, migraine headaches, constipation, and fatigue. These conditions often simply disappeared. And people's energy levels increased markedly, a welcome change for everyone.

Even more remarkable are the women who regained their youthful hormone levels and saw dramatic reversals of thinning or graying hair, skin wrinkling, muscular deterioration, and osteoporosis. In fact, many women stated that they had regained their premenopausal youth. Likewise, many men experienced hormonal turnarounds and found that they were no longer impotent or depressed. All of these people were under their own physicians' supervision, so we were able to have a quantified before-and-after analysis of readings including hormone and cholesterol levels, low-density lipoproteins, and triglycerides. We also evaluated blood pressure and measured body fat percentages. All of this record-keeping proved that the benefits of the program were not psychological, or merely anecdotal or placebo-effect improvements. These were real, hard, objective results.

How exactly does juicing help produce these changes? The green juices cleanse and detoxify the body, while the reds facilitate the repair of DNA. In cases where participants are diabetic, we replace the red juices with concentrated fruit and vegetables powders that are sugar-free. The ultimate healing ingredients are the chlorophyll, the myriad phytochemicals, the antioxidants, and the trace elements that are part of all the fresh organic juices.

The bottom line is that we now have the power to prevent most of the illnesses that were once thought to be inevitable as we age. This book is a tool to help you do just that. The recipes included in this book were created with variety, taste, and potency of therapeutic benefit in mind. But you should also understand that the recipes are intended as a starting point only. Feel free to experiment to meet your own needs and your own perception of what your body can accept. You can be as creative as you choose—and as healthy and happy as you want!

—*Gary Null*

The Basics of Juicing

YOU NEED JUST TWO basic tools for juice and shake preparation—a quality centrifugal juicer and a workhorse blender. With an average investment of about $350, you will be set for all your juicing joys. There are a number of good juicers on the market, but make sure to pick one that has a stable motor and low heat generation. If the juicer overheats, it can kill vital enzymes and decrease the digestive value of the preparations. The stability of the mechanism is more important than the number of r.p.m.s (revolutions per minute) the juicer boasts. The more efficiently pulp can be shredded and ejected from the unit, the less possibility there is of clogging and overheating. Also, choose a juicer that you can confidently clean with ease on a daily basis. If the thought of cleaning each time prevents you from using it, you'll never juice!

A workhorse blender can be any name brand that has a good warrantee policy because, if you take my advice, which I hope you will, you'll use this unit often enough to take advantage of it. Always have a back-up blender or at least a back-up pitcher in case of breakage. Despite the fact that they can break if dropped, I still prefer the glass blender pitchers because they are stronger and easier to clean than the plastic models.

I recommend you try to purchase produce in four-day intervals to allow adequate time for ripening. Always choose organic fruits and vegetables. Because I believe in using the whole food, most of the recipes in this book allow for the peel and skin to remain on the fruits and vegetables when pushing them through the juicer, unless noted otherwise. Much of the nutritional value from most fruits and vegetables exists in the outer layer. A few exceptions are pineapples, watermelon, cantaloupe, papayas, bananas, and mangoes. In most cases, unless specified otherwise, even the seeds should be juiced.

Fruits and vegetables can all be pushed through in one session. Run the drier fruits and vegetables through first and the juicier ones last. This process will allow the juice to flush away pulp that may have accumulated on the centrifugal screen.

If you have a high-quality juicer that ejects the pulp efficiently, you can even juice wheatgrass. You can purchase trays or blocks of wheatgrass, which can be harvested by cutting the blades down to the root. Take the harvested blades and squeeze them into a ball with your hands. When the grass is concentrated in this way, the juicer can easily grab on to the material and process the wheatgrass into juice. You will actually get a more nutritious juice by this method in comparison to a wheatgrass press because with the centrifugal method more of the cellulose and chlorophyll are removed, leaving you with a concentrated liquid. This liquid can then be watered down to taste. Remember, in order to juice wheatgrass with the centrifugal method, you must have a very stable high-pulp ejection unit. These units currently average $350.

Juices

and

Shakes

AntiOxidant Supreme

½ honeydew, cubed (with skin)
15 grapes with seeds, any color
¼ cup red wine without sulfites, preferably non-alcoholic
2 tablespoons aloe-vera concentrate

1 Push the honeydew and grapes through the juicer.

2 Add the wine and aloe-vera concentrate to the juice mixture, and stir well.

3 Serve immediately.

MAKES 1–1½ CUPS

Apple Pear Gingerale

8 large apples, cored and quartered
8 large pears, cored and quartered
4 ounces fresh ginger root, sliced into ½-inch pieces
2 cups sparkling mineral water
16–20 ice cubes

1 Push the apples, pears, and ginger through the juicer.

2 In a large pitcher, combine the juice mixture and mineral water. Stir together until well combined.

3 Pour into glasses filled with ice, and serve immediately.

MAKES 11 CUPS

Apple Sprouts

4 apples, cored and quartered
2 yams, cubed
½ cup alfalfa sprouts

1 Push all the ingredients through the juicer. Stir well.

2 Serve immediately.

MAKES 4 CUPS

Baby Food Juice

THIS IS A TASTY JUICE THAT BABIES SEEM TO LOVE. IT IS HIGH IN VITAMIN C AND OTHER ANTIOXIDANTS. THIS RECIPE YIELDS ABOUT 1 ½ CUPS OF DILUTED JUICE, SO YOU CAN SERVE IT OVER THE COURSE OF 1–2 DAYS.

1 carrot, peeled, tops removed
½ cup cubed cantaloupe without rind
1 cup purified water

1 Push the carrots and cantaloupe through the juicer.

2 Combine the water and juice mixture. Stir well. (Diluted juice is easier to digest.)

3 Keep refrigerated, and serve over the course of 1–2 days.

MAKES 1 ½ CUPS

Beauty

1 medium cucumber, cut in slices
3 medium parsnips, cubed
3 large carrots, cut in slices, tops removed
1 large pineapple with rind, cubed

1 Push all the ingredients through the juicer. Stir juice well.

2 Serve immediately.

MAKES 5 CUPS

The Big Cleanse

WHEATGRASS CAN BE JUICED BY USING A WHEATGRASS PRESS. YOU CAN ALSO MAKE WHEATGRASS JUICE BY SQUEEZING THE GRASS INTO CLUSTERS WITH YOUR HANDS AND JUICING THESE CLUSTERS THROUGH A TRADITIONAL FRUIT AND VEG-ETABLE JUICER.

2 ounces wheatgrass juice
½ clove garlic, peeled
2 cups chopped collard greens
2 cups chopped cauliflower
½ cup cubed red beet
1 cup chopped chard
2 large apples, cored and quartered

1 Push all the ingredients through the juicer, except wheatgrass juice.

2 Add wheatgrass juice to the juice mixture, and stir well.

3 Serve immediately.

MAKES 1 ½–2 CUPS

Brain Juice

1½ cups green beans
½ head of organic cabbage, shredded
2 cups chopped collard greens
1 cup chopped spinach
2 medium peaches, quartered and pitted
3 oranges, peeled and quartered

1 Push all the ingredients through the juicer. Stir juice well.

2 Serve immediately.

MAKES 3–4 CUPS

Brain Power

12 leechi nuts, pitted, skins removed
2 oranges, quartered
2 mangoes, diced and pitted
100 mg ginseng (dried herb or contents of capsule)
100 mg Ginkgo biloba (dried herb or contents of capsule)

1 Push the leechi nuts, orange, and mango through the juicer.

2 Blend the ginseng and ginkgo with the juice mixture in a blender.

3 Serve immediately.

MAKES 1½–2 CUPS

Breath Freshener Juice

THIS CAN ALSO BE USED AS A MOUTHWASH.

1 cup chopped fresh peppermint leaf
5 celery stalks
3 cucumbers, cut in large slices

1 Push all the ingredients through the juicer. Stir juice well.

2 Serve immediately.

MAKES 2 CUPS

Carrot and Soymilk Juice

3 carrots, sliced, tops removed
½ cup non-flavored soymilk

1 Push the carrots through the juicer.

2 Add soymilk to carrot juice, and stir well.

3 Serve immediately.

MAKES 1–1½ CUPS

Carrot, Pineapple, and Strawberry Juice

1 cup of strawberries, hulled and halved
4 carrots, sliced, tops removed
¼ pineapple, cubed, rind removed

1 Push all the ingredients through the juicer in order listed. Stir juice well.

2 Serve immediately.

MAKES 1–2 CUPS

Celery Lane

5 stalks of celery
3 large carrots, sliced, tops removed
½ apple, sliced
ground ginger to taste

1 Push the celery, carrots, and apple through the juicer.

2 Add a dash of ginger to juice mixture to taste. Stir well.

3 Serve immediately.

MAKES 1–1 ½ CUPS

Chlorophyll Ya Up

WHEATGRASS JUICE CAN BE MADE BY USING A WHEATGRASS PRESS, OR YOU CAN
ALSO MAKE IT BY SQUEEZING THE GRASS INTO CLUSTERS WITH YOUR HANDS AND
JUICING THESE CLUSTERS THROUGH A TRADITIONAL FRUIT AND VEGETABLE JUICER.

2 ounces wheatgrass juice
2 cups alfalfa sprouts
2 cups chopped spinach
2 cups chopped collard greens without stems
5 medium asparagus stalks
1 apple, cored and quartered (optional)

1 Push all the ingredients through the juicer, except wheatgrass juice.

2 Add the wheatgrass juice to the juice mixture, and stir well.

3 If the juice has a very bitter taste, juice an apple and stir into the mixture.

4 Serve immediately.

MAKES 4 CUPS

The Color Purple

1 cup grapes with seeds, any color
1 medium beet, cubed
¼ head of red cabbage, chopped
1 cup blueberries

1 Push all the ingredients through the juicer. Stir juice well.

2 Serve immediately.

MAKES 4–5 CUPS

Cranberry Cooler

4 cups purified water
2 decaffeinated green tea bags
4 large oranges, peel removed
2 large limes, peel removed
1 large lemon, peel removed
1 cup unsweetened cranberry juice
2 cups blueberries
¼ cup honey
1 teaspoon ground cinnamon
40 ice cubes
1 large lime, sliced into ¼-inch-thick half-moons, as garnish
(optional)

1 In a small saucepan, add tea bags to the water and simmer over moderate heat, covered, for 8–10 minutes, or until fully brewed. Set aside and allow to cool completely.

2 Push the oranges, 2 limes, and lemon through the juicer.

3 Blend the orange juice mixture, cranberry juice, blueberries, honey, cinnamon, half the ice cubes, and tea in a blender on high speed until well combined.

4 Pour into glasses filled with the remaining ice cubes and garnish with lime slices, if desired.

5 Serve immediately.

MAKES 8 CUPS

Cucumber Coolade

1 large bunch flat-leaf parsley (about ¼ pound)
4 large cucumbers, cut into quarters lengthwise
4 pears, cored and quartered
1-inch piece ginger root

1 Bunch up the parsley and push through the juicer, alternating it with the cucumbers, pears, and ginger. (This process will help push the parsley through more efficiently.) Stir juice well.

2 Serve immediately.

MAKES 4 CUPS

Cucumber, Lime, and Kiwi Divine

3 cucumbers, sliced
1 lime, halved, peel removed
3 kiwis, peeled and quartered
1 teaspoon blackstrap molasses

1 Push the cucumber, lime, and kiwis through the juicer.

2 Blend the blackstrap molasses with the juice mixture in a blender.

3 Serve over ice.

MAKES 1–1½ CUPS

Deep Sea Juicing

1 ounce wakame sea vegetable
1 ounce kombu sea vegetable
1 ounce dulse sea vegetables
2 cups chopped arugula lettuce
2 cups chopped red leaf lettuce
2 cups chopped romaine lettuce
2 apples, cored and quartered

1 Cut the sea vegetables into small pieces and chop in a blender or food processor until very fine.

2 Push the lettuce and apples through the juicer.

3 Add sea veggies to the juice mixture, and stir well.

4 Serve immediately.

MAKES 1 1/2–2 CUPS

Delicious Detox

¼ small watermelon with rind, cubed
2 cups fresh pitted cherries, pre-frozen for about 2 or more hours
2 cups alfalfa sprouts
½ pint blueberries
½ pint raspberries
1 medium peach, pitted and quartered

1 Push all the ingredients through the juicer. Stir juice well.

2 Serve immediately.

MAKES 2 1/2–3 CUPS

Detox Tonic

1 medium watermelon with rind, cubed
8 kiwis, skin removed
2 grapefruits, peeled and quartered
2 limes, peeled and quartered
1 lemon, peeled and quartered

1 Push the watermelon, kiwis, grapefruits, limes, and lemon through the juicer. Stir juice well.

2 Serve immediately.

MAKES 14 CUPS

Eastern Wonder

YOU'LL NEED TO FIND AN ASIAN MARKET OR A SPECIALTY GROCER FOR THESE INGREDIENTS.

½ large radish daikon, peeled and sliced
1 cup Chinese go chi berries
½ medium oriental melon, cubed, rind removed
1-inch piece ginger root
2 ounces Chinese lotus root
½ package bok choy
1 cup Japanese mitsuba with stems and leaves
3 apples, cored and quartered

1 Push all the ingredients through the juicer in the order listed. Stir juice well.

2 Serve immediately.

MAKES 5 CUPS

Enzyme Enhancer

1 medium papaya, cubed
¼ large pineapple, cubed, rind removed
6–10 large strawberries, hulled and halved
¼ medium head of cabbage, chopped
½ small kiwi, quartered

1 Push all the ingredients through the juicer. Stir juice well.

2 Serve immediately.

MAKES 3–4 CUPS

Everglades Punch

1 honeydew melon, rind removed, seeded, and cut into 2-inch pieces
   (about 8 cups)
4 large oranges, peeled and quartered
4 large limes, peeled and quartered
2 large grapefruits, peeled and quartered
2 large lemons, peeled and quartered
4 mangoes, peeled, pitted, and cut into 2-inch pieces
1 cup blueberries
20–40 ice cubes
1 large orange, sliced into ½-inch-thick half-moons, as garnish (optional)

1 Push the melon, 4 oranges, limes, grapefruits, lemons, mangoes, and blueberries through the juicer. Stir juice well.

2 Pour into glasses filled with ice and garnish with orange slices, if desired.

3 Serve immediately.

MAKES 1 GALLON

Eye Essentials

1 cup grapes with seeds, any color
1 medium apricot, pitted and halved
½ pint frozen or room temperature huckleberries
2 medium yams, quartered
1 cup chopped spinach
1 pint blueberries
1 cantaloupe, cubed, rind removed

1 Push all the ingredients through the juicer. Stir juice well.

2 Serve immediately.

MAKES 4–5 CUPS

Fast-Astic Juice

THIS IS AN EXCELLENT JUICE FOR FASTING.

2 medium whole cucumbers, sliced
1 medium apple, cored and quartered
½ medium lemon, quartered
¾ cup grapes with seeds, any color
1 cup watermelon, cubed, rind removed

1 Push all the ingredients through the juicer. Stir juice well.

2 Serve immediately.

MAKES 2½–3 CUPS

Fatigue Buster

3 carrots, sliced in lengths, tops removed
2 cucumbers, sliced
1 pear, cored and quartered
¼ teaspoon bee propolis (If allergic to bee propolis, replace with
   ¼ teaspoon guarana or ginseng powder.)

1 Push the carrots, cucumbers, and pear through the juicer.

2 Add the bee propolis, guarana, or ginseng to the juice mixture, and stir well.

3 Serve immediately.

MAKES 1–1 ½ CUPS

Flavorburst

2 kiwis, quartered
2 passion fruits, quartered
2 tangerines, quartered and peeled
1 grapefruit, quartered and peeled
5 celery stalks, leaves removed

1 Push all the ingredients through the juicer. Stir juice well.

2 Pour over ice, and serve immediately.

MAKES 4–5 CUPS

Fountain of Youth

1 cup green grapes with seeds
1 cup purple grapes with seeds
½ cantaloupe, cubed, rind removed
2 medium zucchini, sliced
1 medium tomato, quartered
2 tablespoons of vegetarian protein powder

1 Push all the ingredients through the juicer, except protein powder.

2 Add the protein powder to the juice mixture, and stir well.

3 Serve immediately.

MAKES 2–3 CUPS

Free Radical Delight

1 cup grapes with seeds, any color
¼ medium cantaloupe, cubed, rind removed
½ cup chopped broccoli
1 cup chopped collard greens (ends cut)
1 cup chopped spinach (ends cut)
3 oranges, quartered

1 Push all the ingredients through the juicer. Stir juice well.

2 Serve immediately.

MAKES 4 CUPS

Gary's Gingerale

1-inch section ginger root
½ large cantaloupe with peel, cubed
½ pint strawberries, hulled and halved
1 medium orange with peel, quartered
4 ounces sparkling water

1 Push all the ingredients through the juicer, except sparkling water.

2 Add the sparkling water to the juice mixture, and stir well.

3 Serve immediately.

MAKES 2 CUPS

Gimme a Juice with Everything

1 apple, cored and quartered
1 cup chopped spinach
1 cup chopped kale
½ cup chopped chard
½ papaya, cubed
2 cloves garlic, peeled
½-inch piece of ginger root
2 tablespoons of protein powder

1 Push all the ingredients through the juicer, except the protein powder.

2 Blend the protein powder with the juice mixture in a blender.

3 Serve immediately.

MAKES 2 CUPS

Gingermint Tea

8 cups purified water
4 decaffeinated peppermint tea bags
4 ounces fresh ginger root, cut into ½-inch pieces
1½ tablespoons honey (optional)
¼ cup freshly squeezed lemon juice
40 ice cubes
1 large lemon, sliced into ¼-inch-thick half-moons, as garnish (optional)
fresh mint, as garnish (optional)

1 In a small saucepan, combine the water, tea bags, and ginger over moderate heat and simmer covered for 8–10 minutes, or until fully brewed. Sir in the honey, if desired, until well combined and set aside to cool completely.

2 In a large pitcher, combine the tea, lemon juice, and ice. Stir together until well combined.

3 Pour into glasses and garnish with lemon slices and fresh mint, if desired.

4 Serve immediately.

MAKES 10 CUPS

Green Pepper Apple Juice

2 green bell peppers, quartered and cored, stems and seeds removed
2 apples, cored and quartered

1 Push the peppers and apples through the juicer. Stir juice well.

2 Serve immediately.

MAKES 1–1 ½ CUPS

Green Power Punch

2 cups chopped kale
2 cups chopped parsley
1 cup chopped spinach
1 medium apple, cored and quartered
1 cup chopped broccoli
½ head of cauliflower, chopped
6 celery stalks

1 Push all the ingredients through the juicer. Stir juice well.

2 Serve immediately.

MAKES 3–3 ½ CUPS

Greens and Grapes

2 cups purple grapes with seeds
2 cups green grapes with seeds
2 cups chopped spinach
2 cups chopped kale
4 ounces purified water

1 Push all the ingredients through the juicer, except water.

2 Add the water to the juice mixture, and stir well.

3 Serve immediately.

MAKES 1 ½–2 CUPS

Guava-Cucumber Juice

2 medium guavas, quartered in lengths
2 small cucumbers, quartered in lengths
1 orange, quartered and peeled

1 Push the guava, cucumber, and orange through the juicer in the order listed. Stir juice well.

2 Serve immediately.

MAKES 1–1 1/2 CUPS

Head Cleaner

2 celery stalks
1 turnip, halved
1 onion, peeled and quartered
3 cloves garlic, peeled
1/4-inch piece of ginger root
3 tablespoons honey

1 Push the onion, garlic, celery, ginger, and turnip through the juicer.

2 Add honey to the juice mixture, and stir well.

3 Serve immediately.

MAKES 1–1 1/2 CUPS

Healthy Smile

1 cup chopped spinach
½ cup chopped parsley
1 medium pineapple, cubed, rind removed
2 medium celery stalks
2 apples, cored and quartered
½ teaspoon CoQ$_{10}$ powder (loose or from capsule)
1 tablespoon lecithin granules (loose or from capsule)

1 Push all the vegetables and fruits through the juicer.

2 Add the CoQ$_{10}$ powder and lecithin granules to the juice mixture, and stir well.

3 Serve immediately.

MAKES 3 ½ CUPS

Honeydew and Yam Juice

½ honeydew melon, cubed, rind removed
2 yams, quartered

1 Push all the ingredients through the juicer, and stir juice well.

2 Serve immediately.

MAKES 2 CUPS

Honey Honey Dandelion

2 apples, cored and quartered
3 cups honeydew melon, cubed, rind removed
1 tablespoon honey
1 cup chopped dandelion greens
1 cup chopped broccoli
1-inch piece ginger root

1 Push all the ingredients through the juicer. Stir juice well.

2 Chill before serving.

MAKES 2 CUPS

Honeymint Cooler

8 cups purified water
4 decaffeinated peppermint tea bags
2 honeydew melons, seeded, peeled, and cubed
2 large limes, peeled and quartered
2 large lemons, peeled and quartered
40 ice cubes
1 large lemon, sliced into ¼-inch-thick half-moons, as garnish (optional)
fresh mint to taste

1 In a small saucepan, combine the water and tea bags over moderate heat and simmer covered for 8–10 minutes, or until fully brewed. Set aside and allow to cool completely.

2 Push the melons, limes, and 2 lemons through the juicer.

3 In a large pitcher, combine the juice mixture, tea, and ice. Stir together until well blended.

4 Pour into glasses and garnish with lemon slices, if desired, and mint.

5 Serve immediately.

MAKES 1 ½ GALLONS

Immune

½ medium garlic clove, peeled
¾ cup red onion, peeled and quartered
1½ cup black or green olives, pitted
4 medium tangerines, peeled and quartered
3 apples, cored and quartered
2 tablespoons eucalyptus honey

1 Push the garlic, onion, olives, tangerines, and apples through the juicer.

2 Blend the eucalyptus honey with juice mixture in a blender.

3 Serve immediately.

MAKES 2–2 ½ CUPS

Joint Power

½ head of small cabbage, any color, chopped
2 oranges, peeled and quartered
¼ cup chopped broccoli
1 cup chopped endive
2 apples, cored and quartered

1 Push all the ingredients through the juicer in the order listed. Stir juice well.

2 Serve immediately.

MAKES 3 CUPS

Ju Ju Juice

2 pints strawberries, hulled and halved
1 cup pineapple, rind removed and cubed
1 medium papaya, peeled and cubed

1 Push all the ingredients through the juicer.

2 Pour over ice, and serve immediately.

MAKES 2½–3 CUPS

Juice from the Ocean

½-inch piece ginger root
1 large cucumber, sliced in lengths
2 celery stalks
1 ounce wakame sea vegetable
1 ounce kombu sea vegetable
1 ounce dulse sea vegetables
2 teaspoons of green vegetable powder

1 Push the ginger, cucumber, celery, and the sea vegetables through the juicer.

2 Blend the green vegetable powder with the juice mixture in a blender.

3 Serve immediately.

MAKES 1–1½ CUPS

King of Chlorophyll
The Greenest Juice in Town

2 cups chopped kale
2 cups chopped spinach
2 celery stalks
2 teaspoons of green vegetable powder

1 Push the kale, spinach, and celery through the juicer.

2 Blend green vegetable powder with the juice mixture in a blender.

3 Serve immediately.

MAKES 1½–2 CUPS

Kiwi Green Cooler

8 cups purified water
4 decaffeinated green tea bags
¼ cup honey (optional)
2 pineapples, rind removed, cored and cubed
16 kiwis, peeled and quartered
4 large limes, peeled and quartered
40 ice cubes
1 large kiwi, sliced into ½-inch-thick cross sections, as garnish
   (optional)
fresh mint to taste

1   In a small saucepan, combine the water and tea bags over
    moderate heat and simmer covered for 8–10 minutes, or until
    fully brewed. Sir in the honey, if desired, until well combined
    and set aside to cool completely.

2   Push the pineapples, 16 kiwis, and limes through the juicer.

3   In a large pitcher, combine the juice mixture, tea, and ice. Stir
    together until well combined.

4   Pour into glasses and garnish with kiwi slices, if desired, and
    mint.

5   Serve immediately.

MAKES 1 ½ GALLONS

Liver Cleanse

1 medium guava, seeded and quartered
2 small artichokes, halved
1¼ cup chopped broccoli
1 medium red pepper, quartered
3 cups chopped celery
3 blood oranges, quartered
10–20 drops liquid milk thistle

1 Push the fruits and vegetables through the juicer.

2 Add the liquid milk thistle to the juice mixture, and stir well.

3 Serve immediately.

MAKES 3 ½–4 CUPS

Liver/Gall Flush

3 cups chopped chopped cabbage, any color
2 apples, cored and quartered
1 cup chopped kale
1 cup chopped spinach
1 ounce aloe-vera concentrate
3 tablespoons olive oil

1 Push the fruits and vegetables through the juicer.

2 Blend aloe-vera concentrate and olive oil with the juice mixture in a blender.

3 Serve immediately.

MAKES 3 CUPS

Melon Boost

½ medium cantaloupe melon, peeled and cubed
1 medium lemon, peeled and quartered
½ small watermelon, cubed
½ teaspoon of vitamin C powder
1 pint raspberries

1 Push the melons and lemon through the juicer.

2 Blend the vitamin C and the raspberries with the juice mixture in a blender.

3 Serve immediately.

MAKES 2–2½ CUPS

Midday Refresher

1 medium cucumber, quartered in length
5 medium celery stalks
1 teaspoon kelp powder
2 medium tomatoes, quartered

1 Push all the ingredients through the juicer.

2 Add kelp powder to juice mixture, and stir well.

3 Serve immediately.

MAKES 2–2½ CUPS

Mister Clean Blood

½ small lemon, quartered
1 small piece organic burdock root
¾ cup dandelion roots
2 cups chopped spinach
1 large pear, cored and quartered
2 apples, cored and quartered
2 ounces aloe-vera concentrate

1 Push the lemon, burdock, dandelion, spinach, pear, and apples through the juicer.

2 Add the aloe-vera concentrate to the juice mixture, and stir well.

3 Serve immediately.

MAKES 3 CUPS

The Morning After

1 medium lemon, peeled and quartered
1 medium lime, peeled and quartered
1 medium cucumber, sliced in length
3 celery stalks
½ teaspoon cayenne pepper

1 Push the lemon, lime, cucumber, and celery through the juicer.

2 Add the cayenne pepper to the juice mixture, and stir well.

3 Serve immediately.

MAKES 2 CUPS

Orange-Berry Lime Slush

16 oranges, peeled and quartered

8 limes, peeled and quartered

2 cups mixed berries (strawberries, raspberries, blackberries, and boysenberries), stems removed

1 large lime, sliced into ¼-inch-thick half-moons, as garnish (optional)

1 Push the oranges, 8 limes, and berries through the juicer. Reserve 1¼ cups juice and set aside in the refrigerator. Pour the remaining juice into 4 ice cube trays and freeze for 1–2 hours or until frozen.

2 Transfer the frozen cubes to a blender or food processor and blend with the refrigerated juice until slush-like in consistency.

3 Pour into tall glasses with straws and garnish with lime slices, if desired.

MAKES 7 CUPS

Papaya the Sailor Man

2 ripe papayas, seeded, peeled, and quartered

½ apple, cored and quartered

1 cup chopped spinach

1 Push all the ingredients through the juicer. Stir juice well.

2 Serve immediately.

MAKES 1–1½ CUPS

The Paradise Drink

1 papaya, peeled, pitted, and quartered
1 orange, peeled and quartered
¼ pineapple, rind removed, cored and quartered
2 tablespoons protein powder
1 slice of lime, as garnish (optional)

1 Push all the ingredients through juicer, except protein powder.

2 Add the protein powder to the juice mixture, and stir well.

3 Pour into a glass and garnish with lime, if desired.

4 Serve immediately.

MAKES 1–1 ½ CUPS

Potato Aid

1 potato, quartered
2 apples, cored and quartered

1 Push the potato and apples through the juicer in order listed, and stir juice well.

2 Serve immediately.

MAKES 1–1 ½ CUPS

Pride of the Detox Juices

6–7 carrots, sliced in lengths
6–7 stalks celery
1 large beet, quartered
1 lemon, quartered
3 garlic cloves, peeled
1-inch piece ginger root
2 tablespoons raw honey

1 Push all the ingredients through the juicer, except honey.

2 Add honey to juice mixture, and stir well.

3 Serve immediately.

MAKES 3 CUPS

Prostate Pro

½ cup choppped parsley
4 medium carrots, cut in lengths, tops removed
2 cups chopped spinach
½ medium apple, cored and quartered
2 tablespoons pumpkin seeds

1 Use the carrots to push the parsley and spinach though the juicer, juicing the carrots in the process.

2 Using a food processor, grind the pumpkin seeds into a very fine powder.

3 Add the pumpkin seed powder to the juice mixture, and stir well.

4 Serve immediately.

MAKES 2–2½ CUPS

Pure Citrus Punch

8 large grapefruits, peeled and cubed
12 large oranges, peeled and cubed
8 large limes, peeled and quartered
4 large lemons, peeled and quartered
16–20 ice cubes

1 Push the grapefruits, oranges, limes, and lemons through the juicer. Stir juice well.

2 Pour into glasses filled with ice, and serve immediately.

MAKES 12 CUPS

Relax

4 celery stalks
3 carrots, sliced in lengths
2 apples, cored and quartered
1-inch piece ginger root
25 mg kava kava capsule
25 mg chamomile capsule
100 mg St. John's wort capsule
50 mg valerian capsule
¼ teaspoon nutmeg
¼ teaspoon cinnamon

1 Push the vegetables and fruits through the juicer.

2 Add the powder from the capsules to the juice mixture, and stir well.

3 Blend the nutmeg and cinnamon with the juice mixture in a blender.

4 Serve immediately.

MAKES 3 CUPS

Relaxer

WHEATGRASS JUICE CAN BE MADE BY USING A WHEATGRASS PRESS. YOU CAN ALSO MAKE WHEATGRASS JUICE BY SQUEEZING THE GRASS INTO CLUSTERS WITH YOUR HANDS AND JUICING THESE CLUSTERS THROUGH A TRADITIONAL FRUIT AND VEGETABLE JUICER.

2 ounces wheatgrass juice
2 pints medium strawberries, hulled

1 medium slice cantaloupe, rind removed
½ pint dandelion flowers and stems
2 tablespoons flaxseed oil
1 tablespoon lecithin

1 Push the fruits and vegetables through the juicer.

2 Add wheatgrass juice, flaxseed oil, and lecithin to the juice mixture, and stir well.

3 Serve immediately.

MAKES 3–3 ½ CUPS

Rock Hard

2 apples, cored and quartered
2 pears, cored and quartered
¼-inch piece ginger root, grated
2 capsules or 100 mg of yohimbe powder

1 Push the apples, pears and ginger through the juicer.

2 Blend yohimbe powder with the juice mixture in a blender.

3 Serve immediately.

MAKES 1–1 ½ CUPS

Roots of Wisdom

3 burdock roots, sliced
2 parsnips, sliced
4 carrots, sliced in lengths
1 cup chopped parsley greens
1 tablespoon blackstrap molasses

1 Push the burdock, parsnips, carrots, and parsley greens through the juicer.

2 Blend the molasses with juice mixture in a blender.

3 Serve immediately.

MAKES 2 CUPS

Skin Elixir

1 cup sliced asparagus
1 cup sliced cucumbers
2 ounces chopped parsley
½ cup pitted black olives
½ apple, cored and quartered
4 medium carrots, sliced in lengths, tops removed
2 ounces coconut milk

1 Push the asparagus, cucumbers, parsley, olives, apples, and carrots through the juicer.

2 Add the coconut milk to the juice mixture, and stir well.

3 Serve immediately.

MAKES 2-3 CUPS

The Spice of Life

1 watermelon, peeled, pitted, and cubed
1 medium papaya, peeled, pitted, and cubed
1 medium kiwi, peeled and quartered
1 medium pear, cored and quartered
1 cup grapes with seeds, any color
½ bunch spinach, chopped
1 cup chopped collard greens
1 medium zucchini, sliced in lengths
½ teaspoon cinnamon

1 Push the fruits and vegetables through the juicer.

2 Blend the cinnamon with the juice mixture in a blender.

3 Serve immediately.

MAKES 3–3½ CUPS

Sprout Power

WHEATGRASS CAN BE JUICED BY USING A WHEATGRASS PRESS. YOU CAN ALSO MAKE WHEATGRASS JUICE BY SQUEEZING THE GRASS INTO CLUSTERS WITH YOUR HANDS AND JUICING THESE CLUSTERS THROUGH A TRADITIONAL FRUIT AND VEGETABLE JUICER.

½ pint sunflower sprouts
½ pint buckwheat sprouts
½ pint alfalfa sprouts
4–5 medium radishes
1 bunch kale, chopped
3 medium apples, cored and quartered
2 ounces wheatgrass juice

1 Push all the ingredients through the juicer, except wheatgrass juice.

2 Add wheatgrass juice to juice mixture, and stir well.

3 Serve immediately.

MAKES 3 CUPS

Stomach Settler

6 celery stalks, top leaves removed
1-inch piece ginger root
12 mint julep leaves with stems
½ cup blueberries
1 medium apple, cored and quartered
2 ounces aloe-vera concentrate
4 ounces sparkling water

1 Use the celery stalks to push the ginger and mint leaves through the juicer, juicing the celery in the process. Set aside juice.

2 Push the blueberries and apples through the juicer.

3 Combine juices, and stir well.

4 Add aloe-vera concentrate to the juice mixture, and stir well.

5 Add water to the juice mixture, and stir well.

6 Serve immediately.

MAKES 2–2 ½ CUPS

Strong Lungs

6 large carrots, sliced in lengths, tops removed
1 apple, cored and quartered
1 avocado, peeled, quartered, and pitted
½ large guava fruit, peeled, seeded, and quartered
3 teaspoons liquid chlorophyll

1 Push the fruits and vegetables through the juicer.

2 Add liquid chlorophyll to the juice mixture, and stir well.

3 Serve immediately.

MAKES 4 CUPS

Summertime Spritzer

1 watermelon, peeled, seeded, and cubed
½ pineapple, rind removed, cored and cubed
¼-inch piece ginger root
½ cup seltzer
¾ cups ice

1 Push the watermelon, pineapple, and ginger through the juicer.

2 Blend seltzer and ice with the juice in a blender.

3 Serve chilled.

MAKES 4 CUPS

Sweet and Sour Watermelon Juice

THIS IS AN EXCELLENT DIURETIC AND DETOXIFIER, ONE OF THE FAVORITE JUICES
AT MY DETOXIFICATION RETREATS.

¼ watermelon, cubed, rind removed
½ lemon, peeled and quartered

1 Push the fruits through the juicer. Stir juice well.

2 Serve immediately.

MAKES 3 CUPS

Sweet Heart

1 medium artichoke heart
1½ cups chopped cabbage, any color
½ pint green beans, tops removed
3 celery stalks
2 large cucumbers, sliced in lengths

1 Push all the ingredients through the juicer. Stir well.

2 Serve immediately.

MAKES 3 ½ CUPS

Veins Be Gone

¼ cup pitted cherries
¼ cup lime, peeled and quartered
1 cup purple grapes with seeds
3 celery stalks
1 carrot, sliced in lengths

1 Push all the ingredients through the juicer. Stir juice well.

2 Serve immediately.

MAKES 2 CUPS

Watermelonade

1 watermelon, peeled and cut into 1-inch cubes
1 large pineapple, peeled, cored, and cut into 1-inch cubes
8 large limes, peeled and quartered
20–24 ice cubes
1 large orange, sliced into ¼-inch-thick half-moons, as garnish (optional)
1 cup watermelon cubes, as garnish (optional)

1 Push 1 cubed watermelon, pineapple, and limes through the juicer. Stir juice well.

2 Pour into tall glasses filled with ice and garnish with watermelon cubes and orange slices, if desired.

3 Serve immediately.

MAKES 1 GALLON

Weight Loss Juice

2 cups chopped kale
1-inch piece ginger root
6 medium carrots, sliced in length
1 cup cubed watermelon
1 cup chopped parsley
½ small lemon, peeled and quartered
1 medium artichoke heart, halved

1 Push all the ingredients through the juicer. Stir juice well.

2 Serve immediately.

MAKES 4–5 CUPS

Weight Reducer

THIS JUICE SHOULD BE CONSUMED THREE TIMES DAILY AS PART OF GARY NULL'S DETOXIFICATION PROTOCOL.

2 apples, cored and quartered
6 celery stalks
1 cucumber, sliced in lengths
4 tablespoons protein powder

1 Push the apple, celery, and cucumber through the juicer.

2 Blend the protein powder with the juice mixture in a blender.

3 Serve immediately.

MAKES 2 CUPS

Yam Juice

1 large yam, quartered
3 oranges or grapefruits, peeled and quartered

1 Push all the ingredients through the juicer. Stir juice well.

2 Serve immediately.

MAKES 2 CUPS

You Say Tomato, I Say Potato

2 tomatoes, quartered
2 potatoes, quartered
⅛ teaspoon cayenne pepper

1 Push the tomatoes and potatoes through the juicer.

2 Add pepper to the juice mixture, and stir well.

3 Serve immediately.

MAKES 1–1½ CUPS

Yummy

3 large cucumbers, sliced in lengths
½ cup blueberries
1 apple, cored and quartered

1 Push all the ingredients through the juicer. Stir juice well.

2 Serve immediately.

MAKES 1½ CUPS

A Trip to Brussels

½ pint Brussels sprouts
4 large cucumbers, sliced in lengths
2 cups chopped cabbage, any color
1½ cup cauliflower
2 medium apples, cored and quartered
1 medium avocado, pitted

1 Push all the ingredients through the juicer, except the avocado.

2 Blend the avocado with the juice mixture in a blender until smooth.

3 Serve immediately.

MAKES 4–5 CUPS

After the Flu Is Gone

8 ounces soy yogurt
½ teaspoon fructo oligo saccharides
2 peeled bananas, frozen
2 cups strawberries, hulled
½ teaspoon powdered probiotic
3 tablespoons raw honey

1 Blend all the ingredients in a blender or food processor until smooth (DO NOT overblend!)

2 Serve immediately.

MAKES 2–3 CUPS

Antioxidant Punch

2 pineapples, rind removed, cored, and cut into 1-inch cubes
4 large limes, peeled and quartered
2 cups unsweetened cranberry juice
1 cup Concord grape juice
1 large lime, sliced into ¼-inch-thick half-moons, as garnish
   (optional)
4 pineapple wedges, sliced ¼-inch-thick fans, as garnish (optional)
24 ice cubes

1 Push the 2 pineapples and 4 limes through the juicer.

2 In a large pitcher or punch bowl, combine the juice mixture, cranberry juice, grape juice, and ice. Stir together until well combined.

3 Pour into glasses, and garnish with lime half-moons and pineapple slices, if desired.

4 Serve immediately.

MAKES 7-8 CUPS

Banana Cream Shake

½ honeydew melon, peeled and cubed
1 banana, peeled
¼ cup agar-agar
½ cup soymilk

1 Push the honeydew through the juicer.

2 Blend the banana, agar-agar, and soymilk with the juice of the honeydew in a blender until smooth.

3 Serve immediately.

MAKES 2 CUPS

Beauty Shake

7 cucumbers, peeled and sliced in lengths
1 lemon, peeled and quartered
1 avocado, peeled and pitted
2 tablespoons aloe-vera concentrate

1 Push the cucumbers and lemon through the juicer.

2 Blend the avocado and aloe-vera concentrate with juice mixture in a blender.

3 Serve immediately.

MAKES 2–3 CUPS

Berries and Cream

1 cup blackberries
1 cup strawberries, hulled
½ cup cranberries
1 cup coconut milk
¼ cup soymilk
½ teaspoon vanilla extract
1 tablespoon protein powder

1 Blend all the ingredients together in a blender.

2 Serve immediately.

MAKES 2½–3 CUPS

Cherry Peach Velvet

24 large peaches, peeled, pitted, and quartered (about 12 cups)
½ large pineapple, rind removed, cored, and cut into 1-inch cubes
   (about 4 cups)
2 lemons, peeled and quartered
2 limes, peeled and quartered
4 cups frozen pitted cherries
4 frozen bananas, peeled
16–20 ice cubes

1. Push the peaches, pineapple, lemons, and limes through the juicer.

2. Blend the cherries, bananas, and ice with the juice mixture in a blender on high speed until smooth.

3. Serve immediately.

MAKES 1 1/2 GALLONS

Cholesterol Reducer

1/2 clove garlic, peeled
2 apples, cored and quartered
2 cups chopped cabbage
1 cup pumpkin, peeled, seeded, and cubed

1. Push the garlic, apple, and cabbage through the juicer.

2. In a food processor, grind the pumpkin.

3. Blend the pumpkin with the juice mixture in a blender.

4. Serve immediately.

MAKES 2–2 1/2 CUPS

Clean Colon

½ cup blueberries
½ large pear, cored and quartered
½ medium potato, quartered
3 large apples, cored and quartered
2 ounces of aloe-vera concentrate
2 tablespoons flaxseeds
2 teaspoons psyllium/bifidus powder
3 tablespoons of raw honey

1 Push the fruits and potato through the juicer.

2 Using a grinder, grind the flaxseeds to a very fine powder.

3 In a blender, on the "whip" setting, blend flaxseeds and psyllium/bifidus with the juice mixture.

4 Serve immediately.

MAKES 3–4 CUPS

Cool Breeze

¼ cup mint julep leaves
2 ounces coconut juice
2 tablespoons carob powder
4 ounces vanilla-flavored rice milk
1 cup granola
1 teaspoon maple syrup
5 ice cubes

1 Push the mint julep leaves through the juicer.

2 Blend the remaining ingredients with the juice mixture in a blender until smooth.

3 Serve immediately.

MAKES 1–1 ½ CUPS

Date Supreme

7 ounces vanilla soymilk
4 dates, pitted

1 Blend soymilk with the dates in a blender until smooth.

2 Serve chilled.

MAKES 1 CUP

Deep Sleeper

1-inch piece ginger root
½ cup basil
1 cup green beans
3 stalks celery
½ head of cabbage, any color, chopped
2 medium bananas, peeled
valerian root extract

1 Push the ginger, basil, green beans, celery, and cabbage through the juicer.

2 Blend the bananas with the juice mixture in a blender until smooth.

3 Add 10–15 drops valerian root extract, and stir well.

4 Serve immediately.

MAKES 3¼ CUPS

Dream Shake

½ cup blueberries
1 pear, cored and quartered
1 banana, peeled
4 tablespoons almond butter
½ cup soymilk
1 teaspoon lecithin

1 Blend all the ingredients in a blender until smooth.

2 Serve immediately.

MAKES 1¼ CUPS

Flax Cruncher

3 tablespoons flaxseeds
1 cup puffed rice
1 cup tofu yogurt
½ cup plain rice milk

1 In a grinder, grind the flaxseeds into a very fine powder.

2 In a blender, chop the puffed rice.

3 Add the flaxseeds and remaining ingredients to blender and blend until smooth.

4 Serve chilled.

MAKES 1–1 ½ CUPS

Friendly Fiber Colon Cleanse
The Ultimate Detox Drink

1 tablespoon flaxseeds
1 papaya, peeled, pitted, and cubed
2 cups cranberries
2 tablespoons psyllium/bifidus powder
1 tablespoon of aloe-vera concentrate

1 In a grinder, grind the flaxseeds into a very fine powder.

2 Blend the flaxseeds with remaining ingredients in a blender until smooth.

3 Serve immediately.

MAKES 1 ½–2 CUPS

Fruity Kazootie

4 apples, cored and quartered
2 teaspoons phytonutrient-rich fruit powder
1 tablespoon aloe-vera concentrate
¼ teaspoon vitamin-C concentrate powder

1 Push the apples through the juicer.

2 Blend juice with remaining ingredients in a blender until smooth.

3 Serve immediately.

MAKES 1–1 ½ CUPS

Fruity Party Punch

½ pint strawberries, hulled
½ pint pitted cherries
1 medium slice cantaloupe
3–4 ounces sparkling water
5–6 ice cubes

1 Blend all the ingredients together in a blender until smooth.

2 Serve immediately.

MAKES 2–2 ½ CUPS

Gary Null's Muscle-Building Shake

*2 heaping tablespoons of protein powder with branched-chain amino
    acids*
1 banana, peeled
8-ounces bottled apple juice
¼ teaspoon allspice

1 Blend all the ingredients together in a blender until smooth.

2 Serve immediately.

MAKES 1–1 ½ CUPS

Gary's "Wake Up" Shake

¼ cup blueberries
¼ cup blackberries
¼ cup black currants
2 tablespoons protein powder
¼ teaspoon ginseng

1 Blend all ingredients together in a blender until smooth.

2 Serve immediately.

MAKES 1–1 ½ CUPS

Groovy Ruby

1 grapefruit, peeled, cut into small chunks
1 pear, cored, cut into small chunks
¾ cup strawberries, hulled
¾ cup blueberries, stemmed, leaves removed
1 teaspoon lecithin
½ cup ice

1 Blend all ingredients together in a blender until smooth.

2 Serve immediately.

MAKES 3 CUPS

Hannah's Smoothie

16 large apples, cored and quartered
16 large peaches, peeled, pitted, and quartered
4 peeled bananas, frozen
¼ cup peanut butter
¼ cup green vegetable powder (optional)
16–20 ice cubes

1 Push the apples through the juicer.

2 Blend the peaches, bananas, peanut butter, green vegetable powder, if desired, and ice with the apple juice in a blender on high speed until smooth and creamy.

3 Serve immediately.

MAKES 10 CUPS

The Healthy Munchy Shake

1½ cups strawberries, stemmed
2 ounces of any healthy nutrition bar
4 ounces vanilla soy frozen dessert
2 peeled bananas, frozen
½ pint blueberries
2 ounces whole blueberry soy yogurt
2 tablespoons carob-flavored protein powder

1 Blend all the ingredients together in a blender or food processor until smooth.

2 Serve immediately.

MAKES 3 CUPS

Immune Movement

1 large Golden Delicious apple, cored and quartered
½ cup cranberries
½ cup blueberries
1 cup dandelion roots and leaves
½ cup soy yogurt
5–10 drops liquid echinacea tincture

1 Use the apple to push the cranberries, blueberries, and dandelion roots through the juicer, juicing the apples in the process.

2 Blend the soy yogurt and echinacea with juice mixture in a blender until smooth.

3 Serve immediately.

MAKES 1½–2 CUPS

Inner Clear

½ *medium organic garlic bulb, peeled*
1 cup cranberries
½ *small onion, peeled and quartered*
1 cup collard greens
½ *pint blackberries*
3 tablespoons raw honey
½ *cup plain soy yogurt*

1 Push the garlic, cranberries, onion, collard greens, and black-berries through the juicer.

2 Blend the raw honey and soy yogurt with the juice mixture until smooth.

3 Serve immediately.

MAKES 1 ½–2 CUPS

Inner Heat

1 cup chopped chard
1 cup chopped spinach
1 avocado, peeled, pitted, and cubed
3 apples, peeled, cored, and quartered
1 tablespoon finely diced peppermint leaves (or peppermint oil, to taste, if desired)
⅛ *teaspoon or 10 mg powdered cayenne pepper*

1 Push the chard and spinach through the juicer.

2 Blend the avocado, peppermint, and cayenne pepper with the juice mixture until smooth. (If preferred, peppermint oil, to taste, may be substituted for the diced peppermint leaves.)

3 Serve immediately.

MAKES 1 ½ CUPS

Kiwi Smoothie

16 large apples, cored and quartered
4 large limes, peeled and quartered
8 large peaches, peeled, pitted, and quartered (about 2 cups)
4 kiwis, peeled and quartered
2 peeled bananas, frozen
1 cup seedless grapes, any color
ground cinnamon to taste
16–20 ice cubes

1 Push the apples and limes through the juicer.

2 Blend the peaches, kiwis, bananas, grapes, cinnamon, and ice with juice mixture in a blender on high speed until smooth and creamy.

3 Serve immediately.

MAKES 12 CUPS

Mango Lassi

¼ cup freshly squeezed lemon juice
1 cup vanilla-flavored rice milk
2 large mangoes, peeled, pitted, and cut into 1-inch cubes
1 eight-ounce container lemon-flavored nondairy yogurt
16–20 ice cubes

1 Blend the lemon juice, rice milk, mangoes, yogurt, and ice in a blender on high speed until smooth and creamy.

2 Serve immediately.

MAKES 3–3 ½ CUPS

The Mighty Berry Smoothie

16 large apples, cored and quartered
2 cups raspberries
2 cups strawberries, hulled
8 peeled bananas, frozen
1 cup protein powder (optional)
2 cups aloe vera juice or water
1 tablespoon powdered vitamin C
16–20 ice cubes

1 Push the apples through the juicer.

2 Blend the raspberries, strawberries, bananas, protein powder, aloe vera juice, vitamin C, and ice with the apple juice in a blender on high speed until smooth and creamy.

3 Serve immediately.

MAKES 12–14 CUPS

Mint Shake

1 carrot, chopped
¼ cup chopped dates
1 cup soymilk
3 peeled bananas, frozen
1 large sprig mint

1 Shred carrot in blender or food processor.

2 Separately chop dates and blend with soymilk, bananas, and shredded carrot.

3 Push the mint through the juicer.

4 Drizzle mint juice on top of the blended mixture.

5 Serve chilled.

MAKES 2–2¼ CUPS

The Most Decadent Health Shake in Town

½ cup nondairy ice cream
½ cup blueberries
½ cup banana, peeled and sliced
2 tablespoons vegetarian protein powder
6 ounces rice milk or soymilk

1 Blend all the ingredients together in a blender until smooth.

2 Serve immediately.

MAKES 2–2½ CUPS

Muscle Performance

1 large pear, cored and quartered
½ large apple, peeled and quartered
1 peeled banana, frozen
3 scoops vegetarian protein powder
7 tablespoons creamy almond butter
½ cup vanilla soy ice cream
10–12 ice cubes

1 Push the pear and apple through the juicer.

2 Separately, blend the banana, protein powder, almond butter, soy ice cream, and ice cubes in a blender or food processor until smooth.

3 Add the juice to the blended mixture and blend until well combined.

4 Serve immediately.

MAKES 3–4 CUPS

Naples Cooler

3 medium cantaloupes, peeled, seeded, and cut into 2-inch cubes
1 quart strawberries, hulled
6 large oranges, peeled and quartered
4 large grapefruits, peeled and quartered
4 limes, peeled and quartered
2 lemons, peeled and quartered
20–24 ice cubes

1 Push all the ingredients through the juicer, except ice. Stir juice well.

2 Pour into tall glasses filled with ice, and serve immediately.

MAKES 1 GALLON

Nuts and Seeds

2½ cups vanilla soymilk
1 pint blueberries
2 peeled bananas, frozen
3 tablespoons soy butter
3 tablespoons almond butter
3 tablespoons cashew butter
3 tablespoons macadamia butter
3 tablespoons sunflower butter

1 Blend soymilk, blueberries, and bananas in a blender or food processor.

2 Add the butters to the blended mixture, and blend until smooth.

3 Serve immediately.

MAKES 3 ½–4 CUPS

Old Man Arthritis

1 large yam, quartered
1 cup cubed pineapple without rind, cored
1 large orange, quartered
1 cup chopped kale
½ cup chopped walnuts

1 Push the yams, pineapple, orange, and kale through the juicer.

2 Blend walnuts with the juice mixture in a blender until the liquid thickens.

3 Serve immediately.

MAKES 3 CUPS

The PC Smoothie

4 large limes, peeled and quartered
1 pineapple, peeled, cored, and quartered
8 large peaches, peeled, pitted, and quartered (about 2 cups)
1 small cantaloupe, peeled, seeded, and cubed (about 2 cups)
4 peeled bananas, frozen
12 ice cubes

1 Push the limes and pineapple through the juicer.

2 Blend the peaches, cantaloupe, bananas, and ice cubes with the juice mixture in a blender on high speed until smooth.

3 Serve immediately.

MAKES 12 CUPS

Phyto-Fiber

¼ *cup oat bran*
¼ *cup hulled buckwheat*
¼ *cup amaranth*
¼ *cup millet*
½ *yam, quartered*
3 *apples, cored and quartered*
2 *bananas, peeled*
3 *tablespoons raw honey*
⅛ *teaspoon cinnamon*

1 Separately cook the oat bran, buckwheat, amaranth, and millet until soft.

2 Push the apples and yam through the juicer.

3 Blend the grains, bananas, honey, and cinnamon with the juice mixture in a blender until smooth.

4 Serve immediately.

MAKES 3–3 ½ CUPS

Soy Wonder

~~~~~~~

2 cups raspberries
1 large ripe peach, peeled, pitted, and quartered
2 peeled bananas, frozen
2 tablespoons soy protein powder
½ cup plain soy yogurt
4 ounces soymilk

1 Push the raspberries and peach through the juicer.

2 Blend the banana, soy protein powder, yogurt, and soymilk
   with the juice mixture until smooth.

3 Serve immediately.

MAKES 3 CUPS

Stamina

~~~~~~~

2 scoops vegetarian protein powder
2 tablespoons almond butter
2 ounces vanilla soymilk
2 ounces soft tofu
1 medium tomato, quartered
1 yam, quartered
3 medium celery stalks
5 ice cubes

1 Blend the protein powder, almond butter, soymilk, and tofu
   in a blender until smooth.

2 Push the tomato, yam, and celery through the juicer.

3 Combine the juice mixture and blended mixture in a shaker with ice, and shake until frothy.

4 Serve immediately.

MAKES 2–2½ CUPS

Strawberry Mint Cooler

8 cups purified water
4 decaffeinated peppermint tea bags
3 tablespoons honey
48 ounces hulled strawberries
2 large limes, peeled and quartered
40 ice cubes
1 large lime, sliced into ¼-inch-thick half-moons, as garnish
  (optional)

1 In a small saucepan, combine the water and tea bags over moderate heat and simmer covered for 8–10 minutes, or until fully brewed. Stir in the honey until well combined and set aside to cool completely.

2 Push the strawberries and 2 limes through the juicer.

3 In a large pitcher, combine the juice mixture, tea, and ice. Stir together until well combined.

4 Pour into glasses and garnish with lime slices, if desired.

5 Serve immediately.

MAKES 11–12 CUPS

Sunrise Oatmeal Shake

3 tablespoons flaxseeds
½ cup rolled oats
1 medium apple, peeled, cored, and quartered
1 medium peach, peeled, pitted, and quartered
2 cups vanilla-flavored rice milk
2 tablespoons grain coffee substitute

1 In a grinder, grind the flaxseeds to a very fine consistency.

2 Separately grind the oats to a very fine consistency.

3 Blend the fruit, rice milk, and grain coffee substitute with the ground oats and flaxseeds, and blend until smooth.

4 Serve immediately.

MAKES 3–4 CUPS

Super VJ Cocktail

1 large bunch flat-leaf parsley (about ¼ pound)
8 large tomatoes, cored and quartered
8 large celery stalks
4 large carrots, tops removed and cut into halves lengthwise
4 yellow bell peppers, cored, seeded, and cut into quarters
4 large limes, peeled
sea salt to taste (about ½ teaspoon)
4 celery stalks, as garnish (optional)
1 large lime, sliced into ¼-inch-thick half-moons, as garnish
   (optional)

1. Bunch up the parsley and push through the juicer, alternating it with the tomatoes, 8 celery stalks, carrots, peppers, and 4 limes.

2. Add salt to the juice mixture, and stir well.

3. Pour into tall glasses filled with ice and garnish with celery stalks and lime slices, if desired.

4. Serve immediately.

MAKES 12 CUPS

Sweet Potato Shake

4 sweet potatos, peeled and cut into 2-inch cubes
4 cups vanilla-flavored rice milk
4 peeled bananas, frozen
1 tablespoon pure vanilla flavor
ground cinnamon to taste
ground nutmeg to taste
16–20 ice cubes

1. To cook the sweet potatoes, place the potato pieces on a steamer set into a large pot filled with 1 inch of purified water. Cook covered over high heat until the potato pieces are tender when a fork is inserted into their centers, about 10–15 minutes. Remove the steamer and run the potatoes under cold water until they are cool.

2. Blend the potatoes, milk, bananas, vanilla, cinnamon, and nutmeg in a blender on high speed until smooth and creamy.

3. Pour into tall glasses filled with ice, and serve immediately.

MAKES 11 CUPS

Tea Shake

THIS IS A GREAT SOURCE OF ANTIOXIDANTS.

1 teaspoon peppermint leaves
1 papaya, peeled, pitted, and cubed
1 mango, peeled, pitted, and cubed
1 banana, peeled and sliced
2 tablespoons protein powder

1 Steep the peppermint leaves in 1 cup hot water for 15 minutes. Allow tea to cool completely and strain.

2 Blend the peppermint tea with the papaya, mango, banana, and protein powder in a blender until smooth.

3 Serve immediately.

MAKES 3 CUPS

Ultra Marathon Energy Shake

2 teaspoons rice protein powder
1 tablespoon soy protein powder
1 banana, peeled
10 ounces bottled apple juice

1 Blend all ingredients together in a blender until smooth.

2 Serve immediately.

MAKES 1 1/2–2 CUPS

Velvety Pecan Milk

THIS IS A GOOD ALTERNATIVE TO COW'S MILK, RICE MILK, OR SOYMILK.

1 cup pecan halves, soaked in 4 cups purified water
4 cups purified water
2 tablespoons honey
1 tablespoon pure almond flavor
2 teaspoons pure vanilla flavor
pinch of salt

1. Soak pecan halves in 4 cups of purified water for 6–8 hours, then discard soaking water and rinse well.

2. Blend the prepared pecans and 4 cups water in a blender on medium speed for 30 seconds, increase speed to high, and continue blending for 1 minute or until homogenous.

3. Transfer the blended pecan mixture to a cheesecloth-lined fine sieve and strain into a medium-sized bowl (squeeze or use a spoon to stir and push the milk through while you pour, since it will be too rich to strain it through without a bit of mashing). Save the pulp for hot cereal, grain dishes, baked goods, or smoothies.

4. Rinse and dry blender, then pour in the strained pecan milk, honey, almond flavor, vanilla flavor, and salt. Blend on high speed until smooth and frothy, about 1 minute.

5. Transfer to a container and refrigerate for 1–2 hours or until chilled before serving.

MAKES 4–6 CUPS

Very Jerry Berry

1 papaya, peeled, pitted, and cubed
1 cup cranberries
2 oranges, peeled and quartered
1 cup coconut milk

1 Push the papaya, cranberries, and oranges through the juicer.

2 Blend the coconut milk with the juice mixture in a blender.

3 Serve immediately.

MAKES 3–4 CUPS

Vision

THIS IS AN EXCELLENT DRINK TO STRENGTHEN NIGHT VISION.

2 pints blueberries
160 mg bilberry extract
1 tablespoon flaxseed oil
1 cup coconut milk

1 Blend all the ingredients together in a blender until smooth and creamy.

2 Serve immediately.

MAKES 2 CUPS

Well-Being

1-inch piece ginger root
1 medium pineapple, peeled, cored, and cubed
3 peeled bananas, frozen
½ cup fennel flowers and stems
1 medium passion fruit
½ teaspoon cayenne pepper

1 Push the ginger root and pineapple through the juicer.

2 Blend the remaining ingredients with the juice mixture in a blender until smooth.

3 Pour over ice, and serve immediately.

MAKES 3–3½ CUPS

Breakfast
Foods

A Live Breakfast Porridge

1 cup quinoa
4 cups purified water
12 large apples, cored and quartered
8 large peaches, peeled, pitted, and sliced (about 4 cups)
2 cups pitted cherries
ground cinnamon to taste

1. In a medium mixing bowl, combine the quinoa and water. Cover and set aside to soak until the quinoa is just tender, but not soft, about 12–24 hours. Discard any excess soaking water, rinse well, drain, and set aside.

2. Push the apples through the juicer.

3. Spoon quinoa into bowls and serve warm or chilled, topped with apple juice, peaches, cherries, and cinnamon.

MAKES 5 SERVINGS

Hearty Oats with Nuts and Raisins

4 pears (1 cup juice)
1 cup purified water
1 cup rolled oats
1 banana, peeled and sliced
¼ cup raisins
¼ cup chopped unsalted black walnuts
½ teaspoon pure vanilla extract
dash of ground cinnamon

1 Push the pears through the juicer. Set aside 1 cup of the juice.

2 In a medium-sized saucepan, combine the water and pear juice, and bring to a boil over high heat.

3 Reduce the heat to medium-low, and stir in the oats. Cook uncovered for 5 minutes, stirring occasionally.

4 Add the remaining ingredients, and cook for an additional 5 minutes, stirring occasionally.

5 Serve hot with unsweetened soymilk.

MAKES 2 SERVINGS

Carrot Sunflower Granola

2 carrots (½ cup pulp)
1 cup rolled oats
½ cup whole unsalted almonds
¼ cup raisins
¼ cup unsalted hulled sunflower seeds
½ cup pure maple syrup
2 teaspoons pure almond extract
½ teaspoon ground cinnamon

1 Preheat the oven to 375°F.

2 Push the carrots through the juicer, and set aside ½ cup of the pulp.

3 In a large mixing bowl, combine the carrot pulp with the remaining ingredients, mixing well.

4 Spread the mixture on a greased cookie sheet, and bake for 15 minutes, or until the top of the mixture turns brown.

5 Serve hot over ice cream or cold with unsweetened soymilk.

MAKES 2 SERVINGS

Barley Cereal with Apples and Spice

4 oranges (1 cup juice)
2 apples (½ cup pulp)
½ cup purified water
⅓ cup pearl barley
⅓ cup whole dried apricots
3 tablespoons pure maple syrup
½ teaspoon ground cinnamon

1 Separately push the oranges and the apples through the juicer. Set aside 1 cup of the orange juice and ½ cup of the apple pulp.

2 In a medium-sized saucepan, combine the orange juice and water, and bring to a boil over high heat.

3 Reduce the heat to medium-low, and stir in the barley. Cook uncovered for 10–15 minutes, stirring occasionally.

4 Add the apple pulp and the remaining ingredients, and cook for an additional 5–10 minutes, stirring occasionally.

5 Serve hot with unsweetened soymilk or juice.

MAKES 2 SERVINGS

Sweet Rice Cream Cereal

4 apples (1 cup juice and 2 tablespoons pulp)
½–¾ cup water
1½ cups unsweetened soymilk
½ cup short-grain brown rice
¼ cup raisins
¼ cup unsalted chopped pecans
2 tablespoons light-colored honey (clover, tupelo, or wildflower)
½ teaspoon pure vanilla extract
¼ ground cinnamon

1 Push the apples through the juicer. Set aside 1 cup of the juice and 2 tablespoons of the pulp.

2 In a large saucepan, combine the apple juice, water, and soymilk, and bring to a boil over high heat.

3 Reduce the heat to low, and stir in the rice. Cover, and continue cooking until the water is absorbed, about 30 minutes.

4 Add the apple pulp and the remaining ingredients, and stir.

5 Serve hot with unsweetened soymilk or juice.

MAKES 2 SERVINGS

Cream of Rice with Peaches and Honey

3 peaches (¾ cup pulp)
1½ cups water
1 cup unsweetened soymilk
⅓ cup cream of brown rice cereal or farina
2 tablespoons light-colored honey (clover, tupelo, or wildflower)
½ cup chopped dates
½ teaspoon pure almond extract
dash of ground nutmeg

1 Push the peaches through the juicer. Set aside ¾ cup of the pulp.

2 In a medium-sized saucepan, combine the water and soymilk, and bring to a boil over high heat.

3 Reduce the heat to medium-low, and stir in the cream of brown rice or farina. Cook uncovered for 3–4 minutes, stirring occasionally.

4 Add the peach pulp and the remaining ingredients, and cook for an additional 3–4 minutes, stirring occasionally.

5 Serve hot with unsweetened soymilk or juice.

MAKES 2 SERVINGS

Tropical Millet Delight

6 apples (1½ cups juice)
1 cup purified water
½ cup millet
¼ cup mashed banana
2 tablespoons chopped dates
1 tablespoon unsweetened flaked coconut
½ teaspoon pure almond extract

1 Push the apples through the juicer. Set aside 1½ cups of the juice.

2 In a large saucepan, combine the water and apple juice, and bring to a boil over high heat.

3 Reduce the heat to medium-low, and stir in the millet. Cook uncovered until the water is absorbed, about 10 minutes.

4 Add the remaining ingredients, and stir.

5 Serve hot with unsweetened soymilk or juice.

MAKES 2 SERVINGS

Cocoa Kasha with Bananas

4 apples (1 cup juice)
1 cup purified water
½ cup unsweetened soymilk
⅓ cup kasha
½ cup mashed banana
½ tablespoon pure unsweetened cocoa powder (unsweetened carob powder may be substituted)
¼ cup pure maple syrup
dash of ground cinnamon

1. Push the apples through the juicer. Set aside 1 cup of the juice.

2. In a medium-sized saucepan, combine the apple juice, water, and soymilk, and bring to a boil over high heat.

3. Reduce the heat to medium-low, and stir in the kasha. Cook uncovered for 3–4 minutes, stirring occasionally.

4. Add the remaining ingredients, and cook for an additional 3–4 minutes, stirring occasionally.

5. Serve hot with unsweetened soymilk or juice.

MAKES 2 SERVINGS

Heavenly Roasted Nuts

1 cup walnuts
1 tablespoon honey
1 teaspoon extra virgin olive oil
1 teaspoon freshly squeezed lemon juice

1. Preheat over to 350°F. Line an 11-by-15–inch cookie sheet with parchment paper and set aside.

2. In a medium-sized mixing bowl, toss together the nuts, honey, oil, and lemon juice until well combined.

3. Evenly spread the nuts on the prepared sheet. Bake on the middle rack of the preheated oven for 8–10 minutes or until the nuts are golden. Remove sheet from the oven and slide the parchment paper to a wire rack until the nuts are completely cool (about 10 minutes).

4. Serve alone or use these as a topping for cereal, salads, non-dairy yogurt, or nondairy frozen dessert.

MAKES ABOUT 1 CUP

Banana Pecan Pancakes

6 apples (1½ cups juice)
1 carrot (¼ cup pulp)
vegetarian egg substitute for 2 eggs
¼ cup pure maple syrup
½ cup purified water

1 cup whole wheat flour
2 teaspoons baking powder
½ cup toasted wheat germ
½ cup sliced bananas
¼ cup unsalted pecans, halved or chopped
2 tablespoons raisins
½ teaspoon ground cinnamon
2 tablespoons cold-pressed flavorless safflower oil

1 Separately push the apples and the carrot through the juicer. Set aside 1½ cups of the apple juice and ¼ cup of the carrot pulp.

2 In a large mixing bowl, combine the apple juice, egg substitute, maple syrup, and water, mixing well.

3 Stir in the flour, baking powder, and wheat germ, mixing well.

4 Stir in the carrot pulp, bananas, pecans, raisins, and cinnamon.

5 For each pancake, heat 1 tablespoon of oil in a small (6- or 8-inch) frying pan over medium heat. When the oil is hot, pour half the batter into the frying pan so that the bottom of the pan is covered with batter. Let the pancake cook for 2–3 minutes, or until the underside is brown.

6 Flip the pancake over, and reduce the heat to low. Cut the pancake into 8 wedges to allow the center to cook. Cook for an additional 2 minutes, or until the center is done.

7 Serve hot with unsweetened soymilk or juice.

MAKES 2 SERVINGS

Tex-Mex Tofu Scrambler

½ cup sunflower seeds

6 tablespoons extra virgin olive oil

4 one-ounce slices "Fakin' Bacon" (tempeh available in healthfood
 stores)

¼ cup lecithin granules (optional)

1 teaspoon onion powder

1 teaspoon dry mustard

1 teaspoon dried basil

½ teaspoon ground turmeric

½ teaspoon ground cumin

½ teaspoon celery salt

½ teaspoon sea salt

1 pound soft tofu, well drained and crumbled

1 cup sliced mushrooms

3 tablespoons tamari soy sauce

1 six-ounce Vidalia onion, peeled and finely chopped

4 large cloves garlic, peeled and finely chopped

1 eight-ounce yellow bell pepper, cored, seeded, and finely chopped

½ cup finely chopped zucchini

1 six-ounce tomato, cored and finely chopped

1 ripe Haas avocado, peeled, halved, pitted, and finely chopped

1 teaspoon balsamic vinegar

½ cup finely chopped fresh cilantro

freshly ground black pepper to taste (optional)

2 large limes, sliced into 1-inch-thick wedges (optional)

1 In a large cast-iron frying pan, over moderate to low heat, roast the sunflower seeds until golden and transfer to a small dish. Set aside.

2 To broil the tempeh, preheat the broiler and brush the above cast-iron frying pan with 2 tablespoons oil. Evenly space the tempeh in the pan and broil in the preheated oven for 5 minutes, or until golden. Remove the pan from the oven, transfer the "bacon" to a paper-towel-lined-plate, and set aside.

3 In a small mixing bowl, combine the lecithin, if desired, onion powder, mustard, basil, turmeric, cumin, celery salt, and sea salt. Stir together until well combined and set aside.

4 In a large mixing bowl, toss together 2 tablespoons of the oil with the tofu and the spice mixture until well combined. Set aside.

5 In the cast-iron frying pan, combine the remaining 2 tablespoons oil with the mushrooms and tamari. Toss together until well mixed and broil in the preheated oven for 5 minutes, or until the mushrooms are golden. Remove the pan from the oven and toss in the prepared tofu, onion, garlic, yellow pepper, zucchini, tomato, avocado, vinegar, cilantro, and black pepper, if desired, until well combined. Return to the broiler and broil, mixing occasionally, until golden, about 10 minutes.

6 Serve hot, garnished with "bacon," sunflower seeds, and lime wedges, if desired, and accompanied by whole-grain toast.

MAKES 4–6 SERVINGS

Soups

Classic Vegetable Stock

1 carrot (¼ cup juice, plus pulp)
1 celery stalk (¼ cup juice, plus pulp)
3 green bell peppers (¼ cup juice, plus pulp)
1¼ cups purified water
¼ cup chopped yellow onions
1 clove garlic, crushed
1 tablespoon extra virgin olive oil
1 teaspoon chopped fresh thyme or ½ teaspoon dried thyme
½ teaspoon celery seeds
1 bay leaf
1 teaspoon sea salt
½ teaspoon black pepper

1 Separately push the carrot, celery, and green peppers through the juicer. Set aside ¼ cup each of the carrot, celery, and green pepper juice. Combine the carrot, celery, and green pepper pulps, and set aside ½ cup.

2 In a medium-sized saucepan, combine the juices and pulp with the remaining ingredients, and bring to a boil over high heat. Reduce the heat to medium-low, and simmer uncovered for 15 minutes.

3 Strain the soup stock through a fine colander or cheesecloth, collecting the liquid.

4 Serve hot as is, or use as a base for other soups.

MAKES 1 SERVING

Vegetable Millet Soup

1 recipe Classic Vegetable Stock (see page 96)
2 cups purified water
½ zucchini, chopped
¼ cup chopped celery
¼ cup chopped carrots
⅛ cup millet

1 In a medium-sized saucepan, combine the stock with the water, and bring to a boil over high heat.

2 Reduce the heat to medium-low, add the remaining ingredients, and simmer uncovered for 10 minutes.

3 Serve hot with whole grain bread.

MAKES 2 SERVINGS

Pasta and White Bean Soup

3 cucumbers (1½ cups juice)
½ head cauliflower, steamed and chilled (½ cup pulp)
¼ cup diced yellow onions
3 tablespoons extra virgin olive oil
¾ cup purified water
1½ cups chopped tomatoes
¾ cup cooked white beans
½ cup chopped escarole or kale
¼ cup chopped celery
¼ cup sliced carrots
¼ cup uncooked whole grain macaroni
2 teaspoons chopped fresh parsley
2 teaspoons chopped fresh basil
½ teaspoon sea salt
½ teaspoon black pepper
1 clove garlic, crushed

1 Separately push the cucumbers and cauliflower through the juicer. Set aside 1½ cups of the cucumber juice and ½ cup of the cauliflower pulp.

2 In a large saucepan, sauté the onion in the oil 2–3 minutes.

3 Add the cucumber juice and water, and bring to boil over high heat. Reduce the heat to medium-low, add the remaining ingredients, and simmer uncovered for 15 minutes, or until the pasta is tender.

4 Serve hot or cold with bread.

MAKES 2–4 SERVINGS

Gingery Bean Soup

2 acorn squash (1 cup juice and ½ cup pulp)
1 small piece ginger root (1 teaspoon juice)
2¾–3 cups purified water
1 cup chopped tomatoes
¼ cup cooked white beans
1 tablespoon chopped fresh cilantro
¼ teaspoon sea salt
⅛ teaspoon black pepper

1 Separately push the squash and ginger through the juicer. Set aside 1 cup of the squash juice, ½ cup of the squash pulp, and 1 teaspoon of the ginger juice.

2 In a medium-sized saucepan, combine the juices and pulp with the remaining ingredients, and bring to a boil over high heat. Reduce the heat to medium-low, and simmer uncovered for 5–10 minutes.

3 Serve hot with whole grain bread.

MAKES 2 SERVINGS

Gingery Carrot Soup

10 medium carrots, tops removed and cut into halves lengthwise
1 piece ginger root, cut into thirds (about 2-inch squares)
1 large lime, peeled
½ cup extra virgin olive oil
1 large Vidalia onion, peeled and finely chopped (about 2 cups)
10 large cloves garlic, peeled and pressed
1 tablespoon + 1 teaspoon grated ginger
1½ teaspoons sea salt
freshly ground black pepper to taste (optional)
2 cups purified water
⅓ cup plain nondairy yogurt
2 tablespoons finely chopped cilantro
1 large lime, sliced into quarters

1 Push the carrots, ginger, and 1 lime through the juicer feed tube. Collect 1 cup of the carrot pulp and all of the carrot juice and set aside.

2 In a medium saucepan, sauté the onion, garlic, and ginger in the oil over moderate heat for 7–8 minutes. When the onion becomes translucent, stir in the carrot juice mixture, carrot pulp, salt, pepper, if desired, and water. Simmer partially covered for 10 minutes.

3 Serve hot or chilled, garnished with a dollop of yogurt, a sprinkling of cilantro, and a lime wedge.

MAKES 6–7 CUPS

Mushroom Barley Soup

8 celery stalks (2 cups juice)
1 cup sliced leeks
2 tablespoons extra virgin olive oil
5½ cups purified water
2 cups sliced mushrooms
1 cup chopped zucchini
½ cup pearl barley
1½ tablespoons chopped fresh dill
1½ teaspoons sea salt
1½ teaspoons black pepper
2 sprigs fresh dill, as garnish (optional)

1 Push the celery through the juicer. Set aside 2 cups of the juice.

2 In a large saucepan, sauté the leeks in the oil until soft.

3 Add the juice, water, mushrooms, zucchini, barley, dill, salt, and pepper, and bring to a boil over high heat. Reduce the heat to medium-low, and simmer uncovered for 25–35 minutes, or until the barley is done.

4 Serve hot, garnished with the dill sprigs, if desired.

MAKES 2 SERVINGS

Celery Potato Soup

1 potato, steamed and chilled (½ cup juice and ½ tablespoon pulp)
2 celery stalks (½ cup juice)
¼ cup chopped leeks
½ cup cubed potatoes
1 tablespoon cold-pressed flavorless safflower oil
1¼ cups unsweetened soymilk
½ teaspoon finely chopped fresh dill
1 teaspoon finely chopped fresh parsley
¼ teaspoon celery seeds
½–¾ teaspoon sea salt
¼–½ teaspoon black pepper
2 sprigs fresh dill, as garnish (optional)

1　Separately juice the potato and celery. Set aside ½ cup of the potato juice, ½ tablespoon of the potato pulp, and ½ cup of the celery juice.

2　In a large saucepan, sauté the leeks and potato cubes in the oil for 3–4 minutes.

3　Add the juices, pulp, soymilk, dill, parsley, celery seeds, salt, and pepper, and bring to a boil over high heat. Reduce the heat to medium-low, and simmer uncovered for 10 minutes, or until the potatoes are tender.

4　Serve hot, garnished with the dill sprigs, if desired.

MAKES 2 SERVINGS

Creamy Tomato Soup

1 butternut squash (½ cup pulp)
½ tomato (¼ cup juice)
¼ cup plus 3 tablespoons plain soy yogurt
¾ cup chopped tomatoes
2 teaspoons chopped fresh dill
¼ teaspoon sea salt
¼ teaspoon black pepper
2 tablespoons plain soy yogurt, as garnish (optional)
2 tablespoons soy Parmesan cheese, as garnish (optional)
2 sprigs fresh dill, as garnish (optional)

1 Separately push the squash and tomato through the juicer. Set aside ½ cup of the squash pulp and ¼ cup of the tomato juice.

2 In a medium-sized saucepan, combine the pulp, juice, and yogurt. Bring to a simmer over medium-low heat, and cook uncovered for 10–15 minutes.

3 Add the chopped tomato, dill, salt, and pepper, and remove from the heat.

4 Serve hot or cold, garnished with the yogurt, Parmesan cheese, and dill sprigs, if desired.

MAKES 2 SERVINGS

Oriental Miso Vegetable Soup

1 leek (¼ cup juice)
3 carrots (¾ cup juice)
2 tablespoons brown rice miso
4 cups purified water
½ cup destemmed shiitake mushrooms
1 cup diced extra firm tofu
¼ cup snow pea pods
¼ cup cubed squash (any type), unpeeled
1 tablespoon toasted (dark) sesame oil
1 tablespoon chopped scallions
1 teaspoon chopped garlic
1 teaspoon chopped fresh cilantro
½ teaspoon grated ginger root
½ teaspoon diced red chili peppers
½ teaspoon hot (spicy) sesame oil

1 Separately push the leek and carrots through the juicer. Set aside ¼ cup of the leek juice and ¾ cup of the carrot juice.

2 In a large saucepan, dissolve the miso in the water, and stir well.

3 Add the juices and remaining ingredients, and bring to a boil over high heat. Reduce the heat to medium-low, and simmer uncovered for 15–20 minutes.

4 Serve hot with whole grain bread.

MAKES 2 SERVINGS

Southwestern Squash Soup

1 butternut squash (1 cup juice)
¼ cup cooked black beans
¼ cup purified water
2 tablespoons plain soy yogurt
½ cup chopped tomatoes
1 teaspoon chopped fresh basil or ½ teaspoon dried basil
½ teaspoon finely chopped jalapeño peppers
½ teaspoon finely chopped fresh cilantro
2 tablespoons plain soy yogurt, as garnish (optional)
2 tablespoons chopped tomatoes, as garnish (optional)
2 sprigs fresh cilantro, as garnish (optional)

1 Push the squash through the juicer. Set aside 1 cup of the juice.

2 In a blender or food processor, combine the black beans with the water, and blend until you have a smooth purée. Set aside ½ cup of the purée.

3 In a medium-sized saucepan, combine the squash juice, black bean purée, and yogurt. Mix thoroughly with a whisk until creamy.

4 Add the tomato, basil, jalapeño pepper, and chopped cilantro, and simmer uncovered over medium-low heat for 5–10 minutes.

5 Serve hot or cold, garnished with the yogurt, tomatoes, and cilantro sprigs, if desired.

MAKES 2 SERVINGS

Some're Cool Gazpacho

8 large tomatoes, cored and quartered
1 large yellow bell pepper, cored, seeded, and finely chopped (about 1⅓ cups)
1 medium Vidalia onion, peeled and finely chopped (about 1 cup)
2 tablespoons finely chopped parsley (flat-leafed preferred) or cilantro
4 large cloves garlic, peeled and pressed
¼ cup freshly squeezed lemon juice (about 1 large lemon)
5 tablespoons extra virgin olive oil
2 teaspoons sea salt
freshly ground black pepper to taste (optional)
⅓ cup plain nondairy yogurt, as garnish (optional)
⅓ cup cherry tomatoes, halved, as garnish (optional)
⅓ cup packed thinly sliced fresh basil leaves, as garnish (optional)

1. Push 4 tomatoes through the juicer. Set aside all of the tomato juice. Dice the remaining 4 tomatoes into ¼-inch cubes.

2. In a large bowl, combine the diced tomatoes, yellow pepper, onion, parsley, and garlic. Drizzle the tomato juice, lemon juice, and olive oil onto the vegetables and gently toss together until well coated. Sprinkle with salt and black pepper, if desired. Toss again.

3. Serve chilled, garnished with a dollop of yogurt, a few cherry tomatoes, and basil leaves, if desired.

MAKES 10 SERVINGS

Chilled Cucumber Mint Soup

2 cucumbers (1 cup juice)
4 celery stalks (1 cup juice)
1 cup plain yogurt
½ cup chopped peeled cucumbers
2 teaspoons finely chopped fresh mint
2 teaspoons chopped fresh parsley
¼ cup diced red bell pepper or pomegranate seeds, as garnish
   (optional)
2 sprigs fresh mint, as garnish (optional)

1 Separately push the cucumbers and celery through the juicer.
Set aside 1 cup of the cucumber juice and 1 cup of the celery
juice.

2 In a medium-sized mixing bowl, combine the juices, yogurt,
cucumber, mint, and parsley. Blend with a whisk until creamy.
Chill for one hour.

3 Serve cold, garnished with the diced red pepper and mint
sprigs, if desired.

MAKES 2 SERVINGS

Papaya Squash Soup

2–3 acorn squash (1¼ cups juice and ½ cup pulp)
2 papaya (1 cup juice)
2½–3 cups purified water
½ teaspoon ground nutmeg
¼ cup papaya slices, as garnish (optional)
¼ cup halved seedless red grapes or pomegranate seeds, as garnish
  (optional)

1 Separately push the squash and papaya through the juicer. Set
   aside 1¼ cups of the squash juice, ½ cup of the squash pulp,
   and 1 cup of the papaya juice.

2 In a medium-sized saucepan, combine the juices, pulp, water,
   and nutmeg, and bring to a boil over high heat. Reduce the
   heat to medium-low, and simmer uncovered for 5–7 minutes.

3 Serve hot or cold, garnished with the papaya slices and red
   grapes, if desired.

MAKES 2 SERVINGS

Cold Cherry Soup

2 cups pitted cherries
1 lemon, peeled and quartered
¼ cup agar-agar
1 cup strawberries, hulled
1 cup blueberries
ground cinnamon to taste, as garnish (optional)
1 orange, sliced into wedges, as garnish (optional)

1. Push the cherries and lemon through the juicer.

2. Blend the strawberries, blueberries, and agar-agar with the juice mixture until well combined.

3. Serve in a bowl, and garnish with cinnamon and orange wedges, if desired.

MAKES 2 CUPS

Cinnamon Fruit Soup

1 butternut squash (½ cup juice and ¾ cup pulp)
2 pears (½ cup juice)
1½ cups unsweetened soymilk
1 teaspoon pure vanilla extract
¾ teaspoon ground cinnamon
6 slices orange, as garnish (optional)
2 sprigs fresh mint, as garnish (optional)

1. Separately push the squash and pears through the juicer. Set aside ½ cup of the squash juice, ¾ cup of the squash pulp, and ½ cup of the pear juice.

2. In a medium-sized saucepan, combine the juices, pulp, soymilk, vanilla extract, and cinnamon, and bring to a boil over high heat. Reduce the heat to medium-low, and simmer uncovered for 4–6 minutes.

3. Serve hot or cold, garnished with the orange slices and mint sprigs, if desired.

MAKES 2 SERVINGS

Papaya Nectar Soup

4 small papayas, peeled, seeded, and cut into 2-inch pieces
  (about 8 cups)
16 large nectarines, pitted and quartered
4 large limes, peeled
⅓ cup lemon-flavored nondairy yogurt
fresh mint sprigs, as garnish (optional)

1 Push papayas, nectarines, and limes through the juicer feed
   tube. Stir juice well.

2 Serve chilled in bowls with a dollop of yogurt and garnished
   with mint sprigs (2 per bowl), if desired.

MAKES 1 GALLON

Salads

Curried Waldorf Salad

½ lemon (1 tablespoon juice)
2 cups diced unpeeled apples
2 cups diced unpeeled pears
1 cup diced celery
1 cup unsalted walnut halves
½ cup raisins
½ cup Curry Mayonnaise (see page 144)

1 Push the lemon through the juicer. Set aside 1 tablespoon of the juice.

2 In a medium-sized mixing bowl, combine the lemon juice with the remaining ingredients, and mix well.

3 Serve chilled or at room temperature.

MAKES 2 SERVINGS

A Chef's Salad

1 head fresh, young romaine lettuce
1 head butter lettuce (about 1½ pounds)
2 cups Savory Croutons (see page 116)
1 recipe "Bacon Bits" (see page 113)
4 ounces Vidalia onion, thinly-sliced
⅓ cup black olives, pitted
1 recipe Creamy Italian Dressing (see page 130)

1 Trim the base of the lettuce and discard any bruised outer leaves. Use the tender inner leaves, keeping the small leaves whole and cutting or tearing the larger outer leaves crosswise into halves or thirds. Wash and dry the greens in a spinner, and transfer to a large bowl.

2 Toss the salad with the desired amount of Creamy Italian Dressing until well coated. Toss briefly with the croutons, "Bacon Bits," onion, and olives, and serve immediately.

MAKES 12 PORTIONS

"Bacon Bits"

1 pound extra-firm tofu, crumbled
¾ cup extra virgin olive oil
1 large clove garlic, peeled and finely chopped
1 teaspoon dried marjoram
1 teaspoon rubbed sage
1 teaspoon dried basil
¼ teaspoon dried oregano
½ teaspoon sea salt
freshly ground black pepper to taste (optional)

1 Preheat the broiler. Line an 11 × 15–inch cookie sheet with parchment paper and set aside.

2 In a medium mixing bowl, toss together the tofu, oil, garlic, marjoram, sage, basil, oregano, salt, and pepper, if desired.

3 Evenly spread the seasoned tofu on the prepared cookie sheet and broil in the preheated oven for 15 minutes, or until golden. For uniformity in broiling, rotate the sheet from front to back halfway through the baking period.

4 Remove the sheet from the oven and cool the bits completely.

5 Toss with salads.

MAKES 3 SERVINGS

Caesar Salad with Thyme Croutons

3 carrots (¾ cup pulp)
4½ cups chopped romaine lettuce
¼ cup Dijon Salad Dressing (see page 131)
¾ cup Thyme Croutons (see page 114)
1½ tablespoons grated soy Parmesan cheese

1 Push the carrots through the juicer. Set aside ¾ cup of the pulp.

2 In a large mixing bowl, toss the carrot pulp with the lettuce.

3 Toss the salad with the desired amount of Dijon Salad Dressing, Thyme Croutons, and soy Parmesan cheese, and serve cold or at room temperature.

MAKES 2 SERVINGS

Thyme Croutons

1 cup whole grain ¾-inch bread cubes
2–4 tablespoons extra virgin olive oil
1½ tablespoons finely chopped fresh thyme
dash of sea salt

1 Preheat the oven to 375°F.

2 In a small mixing bowl, combine all the ingredients and toss.

3 Spread the cubes on an ungreased cookie sheet and bake for 15–20 minutes, or until light brown in color.

4 Toss with salads.

MAKES 1 CUP

Insalata Caesar

2 heads fresh, young romaine lettuce (about 1½ pounds)
2 cups Savory Croutons (see page 116)
4 sheets julienne strips of sushi nori
1 recipe Creamy Caesar Dressing (see page 130)

1 Trim the base of the romaine lettuce and discard any bruised outer leaves. Use the tender inner leaves, keeping the small leaves whole and cutting or tearing the larger outer leaves crosswise into halves or thirds. Wash and dry the greens in a spinner, and transfer to a large bowl.

2 Toss the desired amount of Creamy Caesar Dressing onto the salad greens until well coated. Toss briefly with the croutons, top with nori, and serve immediately.

MAKES 4 SERVINGS

Savory Croutons

2 cups cut-up millet or rice bread, cut into ¾-inch cubes
2 tablespoons extra virgin olive oil
1 tablespoon grated soy Parmesan-style nondairy cheese
¼ teaspoon dried basil
¼ teaspoon dried marjoram
¼ teaspoon dried oregano
sea salt to taste

1 Preheat the oven to 425°F. Line an 11 × 15–inch cookie sheet with parchment paper and set aside.

2 In a medium mixing bowl, toss together the bread, oil, cheese, basil, marjoram, oregano, and salt. Evenly spread the seasoned cubes on the prepared cookie sheet and bake in the preheated oven for 8–10 minutes, or until golden. For uniformity in baking, rotate the sheet front to back halfway through the baking period. Remove the sheet from the oven and cool the croutons completely.

3 Toss with salads.

MAKES 4 SERVINGS

Zesty Tuna Salad

1 carrot (¼ cup pulp)
1 lemon (2 tablespoons juice)
13 ounces canned or cooked fresh tuna
4–5 tablespoons soy mayonnaise
¼ cup unsalted hulled sunflower seeds
¼ cup chopped celery
½ teaspoon sea salt
¼ teaspoon black pepper

1. Separately push the carrot and lemon through the juicer. Set aside ¼ cup of the carrot pulp and 2 tablespoons of the lemon juice.

2. In a medium-sized mixing bowl, flake the tuna with a fork.

3. Add the carrot pulp, lemon juice, and Basic Mayonnaise, and mix.

4. Add the remaining ingredients, and mix.

5. Serve cold over salad greens or as a sandwich filling.

MAKES 2–3 SERVINGS

Mixed Dark Green Salad

2 beets (½ cup pulp)
1 cup chopped radicchio
1 cup chopped Belgian endive
1 cup chopped arugula
1 cup chopped Swiss chard
1 cup unsalted walnut halves
1 recipe Dijon Salad Dressing (see page 131)

1. Push the beets through the juicer. Set aside ½ cup of the pulp.

2. In a large mixing bowl, toss the beet pulp with the radicchio, endive, arugula, Swiss chard, and walnuts.

3. Toss the salad with the desired amount of Dijon Salad Dressing, and serve cold or at room temperature with whole grain bread.

MAKES 2 SERVINGS

Mixed Sprout Salad

2 beets (½ cup pulp)
2 cups lentil sprouts
1 cup radish sprouts
1 cup alfalfa sprouts
1 cup sliced red bell peppers
1 recipe Sesame Orange Dressing (see page 133)

1 Push the beets through the juicer. Set aside ½ cup of the pulp.

2 In a large mixing bowl, toss the beet pulp with the sprouts and peppers.

3 Toss the salad with the desired amount of Sesame Orange Dressing, and serve at room temperature.

MAKES 2 SERVINGS

Cucumber Raita Salad

½ cucumber (¼ cup juice)
2 cups plain soy yogurt
1 tablespoon chopped fresh cilantro
2 teaspoons ground cardamom
½ cup chopped peeled cucumbers
½ cup chopped tomatoes

1. Push the cucumber through the juicer. Set aside ¼ cup of the juice.

2. In a small mixing bowl, combine the cucumber juice with the yogurt, and mix well with a whisk.

3. Stir in the cilantro and cardamom, and mix.

4. Add the chopped cucumbers and tomatoes, and mix.

5. Serve cold or at room temperature with bread or almost any main dish. This salad goes especially well with Matar Paneer (see page 160).

MAKES 2 SERVINGS

Green Bean Salad with Almonds and Dill

2 cups steamed green beans
¼ cup Dill Mayonnaise (see page 144)
¼ cup slivered blanched almonds
1 tablespoon poppy seeds
¼ cup sprigs fresh dill, as garnish (optional)

1. In a medium-sized mixing bowl, toss the beans with the Dill Mayonnaise.

2. Sprinkle the almonds and poppy seeds on top of the bean mixture.

3. Serve cold or at room temperature, garnished with the dill sprigs, if desired.

MAKES 1 SERVING

Red Potato Salad

½ carrot
(1 tablespoon juice and 2 tablespoons pulp)
2 cups diced steamed red potatoes
½ cup chopped celery
2 tablespoons chopped red onions
2 tablespoons extra virgin olive oil
2 teaspoons chopped fresh dill
1 teaspoon celery seeds
1 teaspoon sea salt
½ teaspoon black pepper
⅛–¼ cup soy mayonnaise

1 Push the carrot through the juicer. Set aside 1 tablespoon of the juice and 2 tablespoons of the pulp.

2 In a medium-sized mixing bowl, toss the carrot juice and pulp with the remaining ingredients.

3 Serve cold or at room temperature.

MAKES 2 SERVINGS

Coleslaw with Fresh Dill

1 carrot (¼ cup pulp)
2 lemons (3 tablespoons juice)
2 cups shredded green cabbage
3 tablespoons soy mayonnaise
½ teaspoon prepared mustard
1 tablespoon chopped fresh dill
½ teaspoon sea salt
¼ teaspoon black pepper
dash of apple cider vinegar

1. Separately push the carrot and lemons through the juicer. Set aside ¼ cup of the carrot pulp and 3 tablespoons of the lemon juice.

2. In a medium-sized mixing bowl, toss the carrot pulp and lemon juice with the remaining ingredients.

3. Serve cold as a salad or a sandwich filling.

MAKES 2 SERVINGS

Tomato Garlic Pasta Salad

4 cups cooked whole grain pasta (bow ties, shells, or ziti)
3 cups Tomato Salsa (see page 141)
2 cups steamed broccoli florets
1 cup whole pine nuts

1 In a large mixing bowl, toss the pasta with the remaining ingredients.

2 Serve cold as a main dish or a salad.

MAKES 2 SERVINGS

Beach Salad

3–4 heads fresh, young mixed lettuces (Bibb, endive, and radicchio)
   (about 1½ pounds)
1 large carrot, grated
1 large beet, grated
1 large yellow bell pepper, cored, seeded, and finely chopped
1 five-ounce fennel bulb, thinly sliced
1 recipe Heavenly Roasted Nuts (see page 90)
1 recipe Mixed Citrus Vinaigrette (see page 132)

1 Trim the base of the lettuces and discard any bruised outer leaves. Use the tender inner leaves, keeping the small leaves whole and thinly slicing the larger outer leaves into crosswise strips. Wash and dry the greens in a spinner, and transfer to a large bowl.

2 Drizzle the desired amount of Mixed Citrus Vinaigrette onto the lettuces, carrot, beet, yellow pepper, and fennel to taste and gently toss together until well coated. Toss briefly with the nuts, and serve immediately.

MAKES 12 SERVINGS

Tabouli Salad

3 cups bulghur wheat
1 cup boiling water
3 carrots (¾ cup pulp)
2 lemons (¼ cup juice)
½ cup raisins
½ cup finely chopped fresh parsley
½ cup chopped unsalted cashews
¼ cup sliced scallions
2–3 tablespoons tamari soy sauce

1 In a large mixing bowl, pour the boiling water over the bulghur wheat. Cover the bowl with a towel, and let it stand for 30 minutes. Drain off any excess liquid.

2 Separately push the carrots and lemons through the juicer. Set aside ¾ cup of the carrot pulp and ¼ cup of the lemon juice.

3 In a large mixing bowl, combine the carrot pulp, lemon juice, and bulghur wheat with the remaining ingredients. Mix well, and drain off any excess liquid.

4 Serve cold or at room temperature with whole grain bread.

MAKES 2 SERVINGS

Nature's Total Salad

2 heads fresh, young romaine lettuce (about 1½ pounds)
½ pound sunflower sprouts
2 ripe Haas avocados, peeled, halved pitted, and sliced
1 large cucumber, halved, seeded, and thinly sliced
1 cup cooked millet
½ cup unsalted roasted cashews
1 recipe Lemon Garlic Dressing (see page 132)

1 Trim the base of the lettuces and discard any bruised outer leaves. Use the tender inner leaves, keeping the small leaves whole and cutting or tearing the larger outer leaves crosswise into halves or thirds. Wash and dry the greens and sunflower sprouts in a spinner, and transfer to a large bowl.

2 Drizzle the desired amount of Lemon Garlic Dressing onto the lettuce, sprouts, avocados, cucumber, and millet and gently toss together until well coated. Toss briefly with the cashews, and serve immediately.

MAKES 4–5 SERVINGS

Succotash Salad

About 4 quarts pure water
1 twelve-ounce package quinoa macaroni
½ cup extra virgin olive oil
2 large Vidalia onions, peeled and thinly sliced
1 small kuri squash, seeded and chopped into ¼-inch pieces
*   (about 2 cups)*
½ pound extra-firm tofu (crumbled)
1 ten-ounce package frozen lima beans
2 cups fresh corn kernels (about 3–4 ears)
1 six-ounce can pitted black olives, sliced

1 large red bell pepper, cored, seeded, and diced
4 large celery stalks, finely chopped
½ cup chopped parsley (curly leafed preferred)
½ cup freshly squeezed lemon juice
1 tablespoon + 1 teaspoon sea salt
1 tablespoon dried basil
freshly ground black pepper to taste (optional)
sweet relish to taste
paprika, as garnish (optional)

1 In a large pot, bring the water to a rolling boil. Stir the macaroni into the water and cook until the pasta is just tender, but not soft, about 4–5 minutes. Transfer to a colander, drain, and place in a large mixing bowl to cool.

2 While the pasta is cooking, in a large saucepan sauté the onions in the oil over moderate heat for 6 –8 minutes or until tender. Remove the onions from heat and gently toss into the cooked pasta until well coated.

3 Place the kuri squash pieces on a steamer set into a large pot filled with 1 inch of pure water. Cook covered over moderate to high heat until the squash is tender when a fork is inserted into its center, about 8 minutes. Remove the squash from the steamer and gently toss into the macaroni mixture.

4 Add the tofu, lima beans, and corn to the steamer and cook covered for 10 minutes or until the lima beans are hot. Remove the tofu, lima beans, and corn from the steamer and gently toss into the macaroni mixture.

5 Add the olives, red pepper, celery, parsley, lemon juice, salt, basil, black pepper, if desired, and relish to the macaroni and gently toss together until well coated. Serve warm or chilled garnished with a sprinkling of paprika, if desired.

MAKES 4–5 SERVINGS

Tempeh "Turkey" Salad

About 4 quarts pure water
1 twelve-ounce package three-grain tempeh, crumbled
½ cup sunflower seeds
¾ cup carrot pulp (about 2 large carrots)
1 large stalk celery, finely chopped
¼ cup finely chopped onion
¼ cup finely chopped parsley (curly leafed preferred)
2 large cloves garlic, peeled and finely chopped
¼ cup soy mayonnaise
2 tablespoons extra virgin olive oil
2 tablespoons freshly squeezed lemon juice (about ½ lemon)
1 tablespoon + 1 teaspoon sea salt
1 tablespoon + 1 teaspoon tamari soy sauce
1 teaspoon dried basil
freshly ground black pepper to taste (optional)
paprika, as garnish (optional)

1   Place the tempeh on a steamer set into a large pot filled with 1 inch of pure water. Cook covered over moderate to high heat until the tempeh is tender when a fork is inserted into its center, about 10 minutes. Remove the tempeh from the steamer and transfer to a large mixing bowl.

2   While the tempeh is cooking, in a small saucepan sauté the sunflower seeds over moderate heat for 4–5 minutes or until golden. Remove from heat and gently toss into the tempeh mixture until well combined.

3 Add the carrot pulp, celery, onion, parsley, garlic, soy mayonnaise, olive oil, lemon juice, salt, tamari, basil, and black pepper, if desired. Gently toss together until well coated. Serve warm or chilled, garnished with a sprinkling of paprika, if desired.

MAKES 4 SERVINGS

Summer Fruit Salad

½ apple (2 teaspoons juice)
½ lemon (1½ teaspoons juice)
1 cup diced peeled peaches
½ cup blueberries
½ cup strawberries
½ cup raspberries
½ teaspoon pure almond extract

1 Separately push the apple and lemon through the juicer. Set aside 2 teaspoons of the apple juice and 1½ teaspoons of the lemon juice.

2 In a medium-sized mixing bowl, combine the juices with the remaining ingredients, and mix well.

3 Serve cold.

MAKES 2 SERVINGS

Blackberry Nectarine Fruit Salad

1 large cantaloupe, peeled, seeded, and cut into 1-inch pieces (about 4 cups)
8 large nectarines, pitted and sliced (about 4 cups)
4 cups blackberries
1 tablespoon freshly squeezed lemon juice
3 tablespoons freshly squeezed lime juice
2 tablespoons powdered brown rice syrup (optional)

1 In a large bowl, combine the cantaloupe, nectarines, and blackberries.

2 Drizzle the lemon juice and lime juice onto the fruit and gently toss together until well coated.

3 Spoon into small bowls, sprinkle with powdered, syrup, if desired, and serve.

MAKES 4–6 SERVINGS

Dressings, Sauces, Dips, and Spreads

Creamy Caesar Dressing

¼ cup extra virgin olive oil
¼ cup purified water
¼ cup tahini
¼ cup silken tofu
¼ cup freshly squeezed lemon juice (about 1 large lemon)
1 teaspoon tamari soy sauce
2 tablespoons chopped parsley
1 large clove garlic, peeled and finely chopped
¼ teaspoon dried basil
¼ teaspoon paprika
¼ teaspoon sea salt

1 Blend the oil, water, tahini, tofu, lemon juice, soy sauce, parsley, garlic, basil, paprika, and salt on medium speed for 3 minutes or until smooth and creamy.

2 Serve over salads.

MAKES ABOUT 1 ¼ CUPS

Creamy Italian Dressing

1 cup silken tofu
½ cup extra virgin olive oil
½ cup freshly squeezed lemon juice (about 2 large lemons)
¼ cup parsley, chopped
2 large cloves garlic, peeled and finely chopped
16 fresh basil leaves
½ teaspoon sea salt
freshly ground black pepper to taste (optional)

1 Blend the tofu, oil, lemon juice, parsley, garlic, basil, salt, and pepper, if desired, on medium speed for 3 minutes or until smooth and creamy.

2 Serve over salads.

MAKES ABOUT 2 CUPS

Dijon Salad Dressing

¾ cup cold-pressed flavorless safflower oil
6 tablespoons purified water
3 tablespoons prepared Dijon mustard
3 tablespoons apple cider vinegar
1 teaspoon finely chopped fresh herbs (chives, basil, and/or parsley)
¼ teaspoon sea salt
¼ teaspoon black pepper

1 In a small mixing bowl, combine all the ingredients, and mix well with a fork or whisk.

2 Serve over salads.

MAKES 1 CUP

Lemon Garlic Dressing

½ cup extra virgin olive oil
½ cup freshly squeezed lemon juice (about 2 large lemons)
¼ cup chopped parsley
2 large cloves garlic, peeled and finely chopped
2 teaspoons sea salt
freshly ground black pepper to taste (optional)

1 Blend the oil, lemon juice, parsley, garlic, salt, and pepper in a blender on medium speed until well combined.

2 Serve over salads.

MAKES ABOUT 1 ¼ CUP

Mixed Citrus Vinaigrette

¼ cup extra virgin olive oil
¼ cup freshly squeezed lemon juice (1 large lemon)
¼ cup freshly squeezed lime juice (1 large lime)
¼ cup freshly squeezed orange juice (1 large orange)
sea salt to taste
freshly ground black pepper to taste (optional)

1 Blend the oil, lemon juice, lime juice, orange juice, salt and black pepper if desired, in a blender on medium speed until well combined.

2 Serve over salads.

MAKES 1 CUP

Sesame Orange Dressing

3 oranges (¾ cup juice)
¼ cup toasted (dark) sesame oil
3 tablespoons sesame seeds
2 tablespoons hot (spicy) sesame oil

1 Push the oranges through the juicer. Set aside ¾ cup of the juice.

2 In a small mixing bowl, combine the orange juice with the remaining ingredients, and mix well.

3 Serve cold or at room temperature over salads.

MAKES 1¼ CUPS

Tomato Salad Dressing

1 tomato (½ cup juice)
2 lemons (3 tablespoons juice)
½ cup extra virgin olive oil
1 teaspoon chopped fresh basil or ½ teaspoon dried basil
½ teaspoon chopped fresh oregano or ¼ teaspoon dried oregano
1 clove garlic, crushed

1 Separately push the tomato and lemons through the juicer. Set aside ½ cup of the tomato juice and 3 tablespoons of the lemon juice.

2 In a blender or food processor, combine the juices with the remaining ingredients, and blend for 2 minutes, or until smooth.

3 Serve at room temperature over salads.

MAKES 1¼ CUPS

Sunflower Salad Dressing

2 lemons (¼ cup juice)
¼ cup unsalted hulled sunflower seeds
½ cup extra virgin olive oil
½ cup soft tofu
1–2 tablespoons purified water
1 tablespoon tamari soy sauce
1 teaspoon chopped fresh basil or ½ teaspoon dried basil
1 teaspoon chopped fresh thyme or ½ teaspoon dried thyme

1 Push the lemons through the juicer. Set aside ¼ cup of the juice.

2 Grind the sunflower seeds in a food mill or food processor.

3 In a blender or food processor, combine the lemon juice and ground sunflower seeds with the remaining ingredients, and blend for 2 minutes, or until smooth.

4 Serve cold over salads or with raw vegetables.

MAKES 1¼ CUPS

Cilantro Mint Dressing

4 lemons (½ cup juice)
1 cup finely chopped fresh cilantro
3 tablespoons water
1½ tablespoons finely chopped fresh mint
1½ teaspoons finely chopped green chili peppers

1. Push the lemons through the juicer. Set aside ½ cup of the juice.

2. In a small mixing bowl, combine the lemon juice with the remaining ingredients, and mix well.

3. Serve cold over salads. This dressing is especially good with Cucumber Raita Salad (see page 118) and unleavened bread.

MAKES 1 ½ CUPS

Tahini Garbanzo Bean Dressing

2 lemons (3 tablespoons juice)
⅞ cup cooked garbanzo beans (chickpeas)
⅛ cup water
¼ cup sesame tahini
1 clove garlic, crushed
¼ teaspoon sea salt

1. Push the lemons through the juicer. Set aside 3 tablespoons of the juice.

2. In a blender or food processor, combine the garbanzo beans and water, and blend until you have a smooth purée. Set aside 1 cup of the purée.

3. In a small mixing bowl, combine the lemon juice and garbanzo bean purée with the remaining ingredients, and blend with a whisk until smooth.

4. Serve at room temperature over salads, vegetables, brown rice, or whole grain pasta.

MAKES 1 ¼ CUPS

Zesty Tomato Sauce

2 tomatoes (1 cup juice)
¼ cup chopped green bell peppers
2 tablespoons chopped yellow onions
¼ cup extra virgin olive oil
2½ cups chopped tomatoes
1 tablespoon tomato paste
1 tablespoon finely chopped fresh basil
1 clove garlic, crushed
½ teaspoon sea salt
½ teaspoon black pepper

1 Push the 2 tomatoes through the juicer. Set aside 1 cup of the juice.

2 In a medium-sized saucepan, sauté the green pepper and onion in the oil for 5 minutes.

3 Add the tomato juice and the remaining ingredients, and simmer over medium-low heat for 15–20 minutes.

4 Serve hot over whole grain pasta.

MAKES 4 CUPS

Cilantro Pesto Sauce

1 large bunch fresh parsley (¾ cup pulp, plus juice)
1 small bunch fresh cilantro (¼ cup pulp, plus juice)
2 tablespoons ground or whole unsalted walnuts or walnut butter
½ cup extra virgin olive oil
1 clove garlic, minced
½ teaspoon sea salt
* easpoon black pepper*

1. Separately push the parsley and cilantro through the juicer. Set aside ¾ of the parsley pulp and ¼ cup of the cilantro pulp. Combine the parsley and cilantro juices, and set aside 1 tablespoon.

2. In a blender or food processor, combine the parsley pulp, cilantro pulp, and mixed juices with the remaining ingredients, and blend for 2 minutes, or until smooth.

3. Serve at room temperature over vegetables or whole grain pasta.

MAKES 1 CUP

Curried Orange Sauce

1 orange (¼ cup juice)
⅞ cup cooked garbanzo beans (chickpeas)
⅛ cup water
1 teaspoon curry powder
¼ teaspoon sea salt

1. Push the orange through the juicer. Set aside ¼ cup of the juice.

2. In a blender or food processor, combine the garbanzo beans and water, and blend until you have a smooth purée. Set aside 1 cup of the purée.

3. In a small mixing bowl, combine the orange juice and garbanzo bean purée with the remaining ingredients, and blend with a whisk until smooth.

4. Serve hot or cold over vegetables, brown rice, or whole grain pasta.

MAKES 1¼ CUPS

Walnut Pesto Sauce

1 large bunch fresh parsley (¾ cup pulp, plus juice)
1 small bunch fresh basil (¼ cup pulp, plus juice)
2 tablespoons ground or whole unsalted walnuts or walnut butter
½ cup extra virgin olive oil
1 clove garlic, minced
½ teaspoon sea salt
½ teaspoon black pepper

1 Separately push the parsley and basil through the juicer. Set aside ¾ cup of the parsley pulp and ¼ cup of the basil pulp. Combine the parsley and basil juices, and set aside 1 tablespoon.

2 In a blender or food processor, combine the parsley pulp, basil pulp, and mixed juices with the remaining ingredients, and blend for 2 minutes, or until smooth.

3 Serve at room temperature over vegetables or whole grain pasta.

MAKES 1 CUP

Guacamole and Bermuda Onion Dip

2 lemons (3 tablespoons juice)
4 sprigs fresh cilantro (1 tablespoon pulp)
1 cup mashed avocado
¼ cup silken tofu
¼ teaspoon finely chopped jalapeño peppers
¼ teaspoon sea salt
¼ cup finely chopped red Bermuda onions
¼ cup finely chopped tomatoes

1. Separately push the lemons and cilantro through the juicer. Set aside 3 tablespoons of the lemon juice and 1 tablespoon of the cilantro pulp.

2. In a blender or food processor, combine the lemon juice, cilantro pulp, avocado, tofu, jalapeño peppers, and salt, and blend for 2 minutes, or until smooth.

3. Transfer the mixture to a small mixing bowl, add the remaining ingredients, and mix well with a spoon.

4. Serve cold or at room temperature with raw vegetables or corn chips.

MAKES 1 ¾ CUPS

Tangy Carrot Dip

½ carrot (2 tablespoons juice)
¾ cup soft tofu
½ cup cubed or mashed steamed sweet potatoes
2 tablespoons apple cider vinegar
¼ teaspoon ground cinnamon

1. Push the carrot through the juicer. Set aside 2 tablespoons of the juice.

2. In a blender or food processor, combine the carrot juice with the remaining ingredients, and blend for 2 minutes, or until smooth.

3. Serve cold with raw vegetables.

MAKES 1 ½ CUPS

Lemony Hummus

5 lemons (½ cup plus 2 tablespoons juice)
1 clove garlic (½ teaspoon pulp)
1½ cups sesame tahini
1 cup cooked garbanzo beans (chickpeas)
¼ cup water
½ teaspoon sea salt

1 Separately push the lemons and garlic through the juicer. Set aside ½ cup plus 2 tablespoons of the lemon juice, and ½ teaspoon of the garlic pulp.

2 In a blender or food processor, combine the lemon juice and garlic pulp with the remaining ingredients, and blend for 2 minutes, or until smooth.

3 Serve cold or at room temperature with raw vegetables or on bread.

MAKES 3 CUPS

Tomato Salsa

6 leaves fresh basil (1½ tablespoons pulp)
2 cups chopped tomatoes
¼ cup extra virgin olive oil
1 tablespoon crushed garlic
1 teaspoon sea salt
½ teaspoon black pepper

1 Push the basil through the juicer. Set aside 1½ tablespoons of the pulp.

2 In a small mixing bowl, combine the basil pulp with the remaining ingredients, and mix.

3 Serve cold or at room temperature with corn chips, on toast, or over whole grain pasta.

MAKES 2¼ CUPS

Sweet Kidney Bean Mash

1 pound sweet potatoes or yams, scrubbed well and cut into 2-inch-
thick slices (about 2 cups)
¼ cup extra virgin olive oil
1 eight-ounce yellow onion, peeled and finely chopped
2 large celery stalks, finely chopped
3 large cloves garlic, peeled and coarsely chopped
1 pound cooked kidney beans, rinsed and drained
¼ cup freshly squeezed lime juice
10 large basil leaves
1 teaspoon sea salt
¾ teaspoon ground cumin
¼ teaspoon ground chili powder
freshly ground black pepper to taste (optional)
8 slices of whole-grain country bread or millet bread, cut ½ inch
thick

1 Place the sweet potato slices onto a steamer set into a large pot
   filled with 1 inch of water. Cook covered over moderate to
   high heat until the potatoes are tender when a fork is inserted
   into their centers, about 15–20 minutes. Remove the steamer
   and run the potatoes under cool water until they can be han-
   dled comfortably. Using a small paring knife, remove and discard the peels.

2 In a medium saucepan, combine the oil, onion, celery, and
   garlic. Sauté over moderate heat for 5–7 minutes, or until the
   onions are translucent.

3 In a food processor, using a metal blade, combine the sautéed vegetables with the sweet potatoes, beans, lime juice, basil leaves, salt, cumin, chili powder, and black pepper, if desired. Process together until smooth and creamy, about 2 minutes. Set aside.

4 Lightly toast the bread on both sides. Spread bread slices with sweet mash and serve warm.

MAKES 4–6 SERVINGS

Basil Mayonnaise

1 large bunch fresh basil (½ cup pulp)
2 cloves garlic (1 teaspoon pulp)
1½ cups soy mayonnaise

1 Separately push the basil and garlic through the juicer. Set aside ½ cup of the basil pulp and 1 teaspoon of the garlic pulp.

2 In a blender or food processor, combine the basil and garlic pulp with the soy mayonnaise, and blend for 2 minutes, or until smooth. Keep refrigerated in a covered glass jar.

3 Serve with raw vegetables.

MAKES 2 CUPS

Dill Mayonnaise

1 large bunch fresh dill (½ cup pulp)
½ lemon (2 teaspoons juice)
1½ cups soy mayonnaise

1 Juice the dill and the lemon. Set aside ½ cup of the dill pulp and 2 teaspoons of the lemon juice.

2 In a blender or food processor, combine the dill pulp and lemon juice with the soy mayonnaise, and blend for 2 minutes, or until smooth. Keep refrigerated in a covered glass jar.

3 Serve with raw vegetables.

MAKES 2 CUPS

Curry Mayonnaise

¾ teaspoon ground cumin
¾ teaspoon ground turmeric
¼ teaspoon mustard powder
¼ teaspoon ground ginger
⅛ teaspoon ground cinnamon
⅛ teaspoon cayenne pepper
1½ cups soy mayonnaise

1 In a blender or food processor, combine all the ingredients, and blend for 2 minutes, or until smooth. Keep refrigerated in a covered glass jar.

2 Serve with raw vegetables.

MAKES 1½ CUPS

Orange Apricot Spread

12 oranges (3 cups juice and ¼ cup pulp)
½ cup chopped dried apricots
¼ cup finely chopped orange peel
¼ cup chopped dates
2 tablespoons apple cider vinegar
1 tablespoon finely chopped red onion
dash of ground allspice

1 Push the oranges through the juicer. Set aside 3 cups juice and ¼ cup pulp.

2 In a medium-sized saucepan, bring the orange juice to a boil over high heat.

3 Reduce the heat to medium-low, add the remaining ingredients, and simmer for 15–20 minutes, or until the mixture reaches the consistency of spreadable preserves. Remove from the heat, and let cool before using.

4 Serve cold or at room temperature with breads and muffins.

MAKES 2 CUPS

Cranberry Chutney

12 apples (3 cups juice and ½ cup pulp)
1 cup cranberries
½ cup chopped dried apricots
4 tablespoons chopped dates
2 tablespoons apple cider vinegar
2 tablespoons diced red onions
¼ teaspoon ground allspice

1 Push the apples through the juicer. Set aside 3 cups of the juice and ½ cup of the pulp.

2 In a small saucepan, bring the apple juice to a boil over high heat.

3 Reduce the heat to medium-low, add the remaining ingredients, and simmer for 15–20 minutes, or until the mixture reaches the consistency of spreadable preserves. Remove from the heat, and let cool before using.

4 Serve cold or at room temperature with any vegetable dish.

MAKES 2 CUPS

Peanut Butter Honey Spread

½ peeled banana, frozen (¼ cup pulp)
1 cup unsalted peanuts
3 tablespoons light-colored honey (clover, tupelo, or wildflower)

1 Push the frozen banana through the juicer. Set aside ¼ cup of the pulp (mashed banana).

2 In a blender, food processor, or food mill, blend the peanuts until they are smooth and creamy.

3 In a small mixing bowl, combine the banana pulp, peanut butter, and honey until well mixed.

4 Serve at room temperature with breads and muffins or fresh fruit slices.

MAKES 1 ¼ CUPS

Basil Herb Oil

4 leaves fresh basil (1 tablespoon pulp)
2 cloves garlic (1 teaspoon pulp)
9 tablespoons extra virgin olive oil
¼ teaspoon sea salt

1 Separately push the basil and garlic through the juicer. Set aside 1 tablespoon of the basil pulp and 1 teaspoon of the garlic pulp.

2 In a small mixing bowl, combine the basil and garlic pulp with the remaining ingredients, and blend with a whisk until smooth.

3 Serve at room temperature with breads and muffins, or toss with hot whole grain pasta.

MAKES ½ CUP

Main
Dishes

Fettucine with Pesto and Tomatoes

1 cup sliced mushrooms
1 cup broccoli florets
3 tablespoons extra virgin olive oil
3 cups cooked whole grain fettucine
1 recipe Walnut Pesto Sauce (see page 138)
1 cup chopped tomatoes
¼ cup grated soy Parmesan cheese, as garnish (optional)

1 In a large saucepan, sauté the mushrooms and broccoli in the oil over high heat for 3–5 minutes.

2 Reduce the heat to low, add the fettucine and Walnut Pesto Sauce, and toss.

3 Add the tomatoes and toss.

4 Serve hot, garnished with soy cheese, if desired.

MAKES 2 SERVINGS

Mushroom Lasagna

4 carrots (1 cup pulp)
4 cups soy ricotta cheese
vegetarian egg substitute for 2 eggs
½ cup grated soy Parmesan cheese
¼ cup chopped fresh parsley
½ teaspoon sea salt
¼ teaspoon black pepper

2 cups broccoli florets
2 cups sliced mushrooms
3 tablespoons extra virgin olive oil
2 cups Zesty Tomato Sauce (see page 136)
1 pound cooked whole grain lasagna noodles
3½ cups shredded soy mozzarella cheese

1 Preheat the oven to 425°F.

2 Push the carrots through the juicer. Set aside 1 cup of the pulp.

3 In a medium-sized mixing bowl, combine the carrot pulp, soy ricotta cheese, egg substitute, soy Parmesan cheese, parsley, salt, and pepper, and mix well with a whisk. Set aside.

4 In a large saucepan, sauté the broccoli and mushrooms in the oil over high heat for 3–5 minutes. Set aside.

5 Spread 1 cup of the Zesty Tomato Sauce on the bottom of an ungreased 12-by-17-inch lasagna pan or baking dish. On top of the sauce, arrange a layer of lasagna noodles, a layer of broccoli and mushrooms, a layer of the soy ricotta mixture, a layer of soy mozzarella cheese, and another layer of noodles. Repeat the layers, ending with additional layers of sauce and soy mozzarella.

6 Cover the lasagna and bake for 45–55 minutes. Let stand for 5 minutes before cutting.

7 Serve hot with a salad and whole grain bread.

MAKES 6–8 SERVINGS

Zesty Italian Pizza

1 cup chopped plum tomatoes with juice
1 packed cup chopped fresh basil
¼ cup chopped sun-dried tomatoes
1 tablespoon Cilantro Pesto Sauce (see page 136)
½ teaspoon sea salt
2 pieces whole wheat pita bread
¾ cup shredded soy mozzarella cheese
½ cup grated soy Parmesan cheese

1 Preheat the oven to 350°F.

2 In a small mixing bowl, combine the plum tomatoes, basil, sun-dried tomatoes, Cilantro Pesto Sauce, and salt, and mix well.

3 Place the pita bread on an ungreased cookie sheet, and spread with the tomato mixture. Sprinkle the top of each pizza with the soy mozzarella and soy Parmesan cheese.

4 Bake the pizzas for 15–20 minutes, or until the top is bubbly.

5 Serve hot with a salad.

MAKES 2 SERVINGS

Mushroom Broccoli Quiche

1 tomato (½ cup juice)
1 large bunch fresh basil (½ cup pulp)
1 cup silken tofu
1 cup Guacamole and Bermuda Onion Dip (see page 138)
¾ cup grated soy Parmesan cheese
2 tablespoons extra virgin olive oil
⅛ teaspoon sea salt
⅛ teaspoon black pepper
1¼ cups thinly sliced broccoli
1¼ cups thinly sliced mushrooms
1 recipe Basic Spelt Crust, prebaked (see page 171)

1 Preheat the oven to 375°F.

2 Separately push the tomato and basil through the juicer. Set aside ½ cup of the tomato juice and ½ cup of the basil pulp.

3 In a blender or food processor, combine the tomato juice, basil pulp, tofu, Guacamole and Bermuda Onion Dip, soy cheese, oil, salt, and pepper, and blend for 1 minute, or until creamy.

4 Arrange the broccoli and mushrooms on the bottom of the prepared Basic Spelt Crust. Pour the tofu mixture over the vegetables.

5 Bake the quiche uncovered for 25–30 minutes, or until the top of the quiche has set and begun to turn light brown in color. Remove the quiche from the oven, and let stand for 5 minutes before cutting.

6 Serve hot with a salad.

MAKES 6–8 SERVINGS

Spicy Texas Chili

4 carrots (1 cup juice)
3 red or green bell peppers (¼ cup juice)
½ cup finely chopped yellow onions
¼ cup extra virgin olive oil
½ eggplant, chopped
½ cup cooked garbanzo beans (chickpeas)
½ cup cooked red kidney beans
½ cup sliced pattypan squash or zucchini
⅓ cup stewed tomatoes
¼ cup chopped green bell peppers
¼ cup corn kernels, fresh or frozen
¼ cup tomato purée
2½ teaspoons chopped green chili peppers
1 clove garlic, crushed

1 Separately push the carrots and the 3 peppers through the juicer. Set aside 1 cup of the carrot juice and ¼ cup of the pepper juice.

2 In a large saucepan, sauté the onions in the oil over high heat until the onions are soft.

3 Add the remaining ingredients to the saucepan, and bring to a boil. Reduce the heat to medium-low, and simmer uncovered for 15–20 minutes, or until the vegetables are tender.

4 Serve hot with spelt bread or whole grain pasta.

MAKES 2 SERVINGS

Curried Red Lentil Stew

2 carrots (½ cup juice)

2 stalks celery (½ cup juice)

1 beet (¼ cup juice)

¼ cup finely chopped yellow onions

2 tablespoons extra virgin olive oil

½ cup finely chopped tomatoes

3¾ cups water

¾ cup dried red lentils

1½ tablespoons finely chopped fresh cilantro

1 teaspoon dried parsley

1 teaspoon dried basil

¾ teaspoon curry powder

1 bay leaf

dash of ground cardamom

1¼ cups assorted frozen vegetables (carrots, broccoli, and/or cauliflower)

1. Separately push the carrots, celery, and beet through the juicer. Set aside ½ cup of the carrot juice, ½ cup of the celery juice, and ¼ cup of the beet juice.

2. In a large saucepan, sauté the onions in the oil over high heat until soft.

3. Reduce the heat to medium-low, add the juices, tomatoes, water, and lentils, and cook uncovered for 15 minutes.

4. Add the cilantro, parsley, basil, curry powder, bay leaf, and cardamom, and cook for an additional 25 minutes.

5. Add the frozen vegetables, and cook, stirring occasionally, for another 15 minutes, or until the vegetables are tender and the lentils are done.

6. Serve hot with brown rice.

MAKES 2 SERVINGS

Lentil Burgers

4 carrots (½ cup pulp)
1 cup cooked red lentils
¼ cup lentil sprouts
¼ cup ground unsalted cashews or cashew butter
2 tablespoons chopped unsalted almonds
1 tablespoon diced yellow onions
2 teaspoons curry powder
½ teaspoon ground coriander
½ teaspoon sea salt
½ cup whole spelt bread crumbs

1. Preheat the oven to 425°F.

2. Push the carrot through the juicer. Set aside ½ cup of the pulp.

3. In a small mixing bowl, combine the carrot pulp with the lentils, lentil sprouts, cashews, almonds, onion, curry powder, coriander, and salt, and mix well.

4. Shape the mixture into 2 patties, coat the patties with the bread crumbs, and place them on an ungreased cookie sheet.

5. Bake the patties for 10 minutes, turn the patties over, and bake for an additional 10–15 minutes.

6. Serve hot in pita bread pockets with Lemony Hummus (see page 140).

MAKES 2 SERVINGS

Halibut with Tomato Salsa

2 eight-ounce halibut steaks
1 recipe Tomato Salsa (see page 141)

1 Preheat the broiler to 550°F.

2 Broil the halibut for 10 minutes, baste with the Tomato Salsa, turn the steaks over, baste again, and broil for an additional 5–7 minutes.

3 Serve with brown rice.

MAKES 2 SERVINGS

Salmon with Teriyaki Sauce

1 small piece ginger root (1 teaspoon pulp)
¼ cup tamari soy sauce
1 clove garlic, crushed
1 tablespoon pure maple syrup
1 teaspoon sweet rice vinegar
2 eight-ounce salmon steaks

1 Preheat the broiler to 550°F.

2 Push the ginger through the juicer. Set aside 1 teaspoon of the pulp.

3 In a small mixing bowl, combine the ginger pulp, soy sauce, garlic, maple syrup, and vinegar, and mix well. Set aside.

4 Broil the salmon for 10 minutes, baste with the sauce in step 3, turn the steaks over, baste again, and broil for an additional 5 minutes.

5 Serve with brown rice.

MAKES 2 SERVINGS

Sole with Walnut Pesto Sauce

2 eight-ounce pieces of filet of sole
1 recipe Walnut Pesto Sauce (see page 138)

1 Preheat the broiler to 550°F.

2 Broil the sole for 10 minutes, baste with the Walnut Pesto Sauce, turn the filets over, baste again, and broil for an additional 5 minutes.

3 Serve with brown rice.

MAKES 2 SERVINGS

Swordfish with Basil Herb Oil

2 eight-ounce swordfish steaks
1 recipe Basil Herb Oil (see page 148)

1 Preheat the broiler to 550°F.

2 Broil the swordfish for 10 minutes, baste with the Basil Herb Oil, turn the steaks over, baste again, and broil for an additional 10 minutes.

3 Serve with brown rice or whole grain pasta.

MAKES 2 SERVINGS

Matar Paneer

1 tomato (½ cup juice)
16 ounces extra-firm tofu, cut into 1-inch cubes
2 tablespoons safflower oil
¾ cup chopped yellow onions
2 cups frozen peas
1 cup chopped tomatoes
¾ cup unsweetened soymilk
3 teaspoons apple cider vinegar
½ cup finely chopped fresh cilantro
2 fresh green chili peppers, finely chopped
3 cloves garlic, crushed
2 teaspoons grated ginger root
1 teaspoon ground coriander
1 teaspoon ground turmeric
¼ teaspoon chili powder
1½ teaspoons sea salt

1 Push the tomato through the juicer. Set aside ½ cup of the juice.

2 In a large frying pan, brown the tofu in the oil over high heat.

3 Add the onions, and sauté for 2–3 minutes, or until the onions are soft.

4 Reduce the heat to medium-low, add the remaining ingredients, and simmer uncovered for an additional 5 minutes.

5 Serve hot with Peas Pillau with Cinnamon (see page 165).

MAKES 4 SERVINGS

Stir-Fried Broccoli with Tempeh and Lemon Threads

5 cups fresh basil (1 cup pulp)
1 small bunch fresh cilantro (¼ cup pulp)
2 lemons (¼ cup juice)
2 cloves garlic (1 teaspoon pulp)
1 lemon
¼ cup tamari soy sauce
1–2 tablespoons whole grain flour
1 tablespoon apple cider vinegar
1 teaspoon chopped red chili peppers
1 teaspoon grated ginger root
2 cups tempeh, cut into 1-inch cubes
¼ cup toasted (dark) sesame oil
2½ cups broccoli florets
¼ cup sliced scallions
1 pint cherry tomatoes

1 Separately push the basil, cilantro, 2 lemons, and garlic through the juicer. Set aside 1 cup of the basil pulp, ¼ cup of the cilantro pulp, ¼ cup of the lemon juice, and 1 teaspoon of the garlic pulp.

2 Peel the remaining lemon, and slice the peel into threads. Set aside 1 tablespoon of the threads.

3 In a blender or food processor, combine the basil, cilantro, and garlic pulp with the lemon juice, soy sauce, flour, vinegar, peppers, and ginger, and blend for 2 minutes.

4 Transfer the basil mixture to a small saucepan, stir in the lemon peel threads, and heat for 4–5 minutes, or until warm.

5 In a large frying pan, brown the tempeh in the oil over medium to high heat.

6 Reduce the heat to medium-low, add the broccoli and scallions, cover, and cook for 2 minutes.

7 Add the tomatoes, and cook uncovered for 1 additional minute.

8 Arrange the tempeh mixture on a serving platter, and pour the heated sauce over the mixture.

9 Serve hot with brown rice.

MAKES 2–3 SERVINGS

Scalloped Autumn Vegetables

10 parsnips (½ cup juice and 2 tablespoons pulp)
1½ cups unsweetened soymilk
2 tablespoons chopped fresh parsley
1 tablespoon cold-pressed flavorless safflower oil
½ teaspoon sea salt
1 teaspoon chopped fresh thyme or ½ teaspoon dried thyme
½ teaspoon chopped fresh rosemary or ¼ teaspoon dried rosemary
1 clove garlic, crushed
1½ cups sliced parsnips
1 cup sliced white potatoes
1 cup sliced acorn squash
½ cup chopped leeks
2 cups grated soy mozzarella cheese (optional)

1   Preheat the oven to 425°F.

2   Push the parsnips through the juicer. Set aside ½ cup of the juice and 2 tablespoons of the pulp.

3   In a small mixing bowl, combine the parsnip juice and pulp, soymilk, parsley, oil, salt, thyme, rosemary, and garlic, and mix well.

4   In a medium-sized mixing bowl, toss together the sliced parsnips, potatoes, squash, and leeks.

5   Arrange the vegetables on the bottom of a greased 9-by-12-inch baking dish or other large glass or ceramic dish. Pour the sauce over the vegetables, and sprinkle on the cheese, if desired. Cover with a glass lid or aluminum foil, and bake for 25 minutes, or until the vegetables are tender.

6   Serve hot with a salad or whole grain pasta.

MAKES 4 SERVINGS

Zesty Cauliflower with Garlic and Tahini

1 recipe Tahini Garbanzo Bean Dressing (see page 135)
1 cup cauliflower florets
1 cup broccoli florets
1 cup sliced red bell peppers
½ cup unsalted whole cashews
½ cup diced red bell pepper, as garnish (optional)
4 sprigs fresh parsley, as garnish (optional)

1 Preheat the oven to 425°F.

2 In a medium-sized mixing bowl, combine the Tahini Garbanzo Bean Dressing, cauliflower, broccoli, sliced red pepper, and cashews, and toss to mix.

3 Pour the mixture into a greased 9-by-12-inch baking dish or other large glass or ceramic dish. Cover with a glass lid or aluminum foil, and bake for 25–35 minutes, or until the cauliflower is tender. (The other vegetables should still be crunchy.)

4 Garnish with the diced red pepper and parsley, if desired, and serve hot or cold with any rice or pasta dish.

MAKES 2 SERVINGS

Peas Pillau with Cinnamon

4 carrots (1 cup juice)
2 teaspoons saffron threads
2 teaspoons water
1 cup uncooked white Basmati rice
3 tablespoons sesame oil
2 cups purified water
1½ cups frozen peas
1 tablespoon ground cardamom
1 stick cinnamon
1 teaspoon sea salt
½ teaspoon black pepper

1 Push the carrots through the juicer. Set aside 1 cup of the juice.

2 Dissolve the saffron threads in the 2 teaspoons of water.

3 In a medium-sized saucepan, sauté the rice in the oil over medium to high heat until the rice is light brown in color.

4 Add the carrot juice, saffron, and 2 cups of water, and bring the mixture to a boil over high heat. Reduce the heat to medium-low, cover, and cook for 12–15 minutes, or until all of the water is absorbed.

5 Stir in the remaining ingredients, and continue cooking until the mixture is hot.

6 Remove the cinnamon stick, and serve hot with Matar Paneer (see page 160) or a salad and whole grain bread.

MAKES 2–4 SERVINGS

Japanese Rice with Shiitake Mushrooms

2-inch piece of ginger root (2 tablespoons juice)
3 tablespoons safflower or other light oil
1½ cups sliced destemmed shiitake mushrooms
1 cup sliced zucchini
1 cup mung bean sprouts, drained
½ cup tamari soy sauce
3 teaspoons sliced scallions
4 cups cooked short-grain brown rice

1 Push the ginger through the juicer. Set aside 2 tablespoons of the juice.

2 In a large frying pan, sauté the mushrooms and zucchini in the oil over high heat until soft.

3 Reduce the heat to medium-low, add the ginger juice, bean sprouts, soy sauce, and scallions, and simmer for 1–2 minutes, or until the mixture has thickened.

4 Spoon the vegetable mixture over the rice, and serve hot.

MAKES 2 SERVINGS

Desserts

Apple Pecan Cobbler

FILLING

2 pears (½ cup juice and ¾ cup pulp)

2 apples (½ cup juice and ¾ cup pulp)

1 orange, peeled (¼ cup juice)

½ lemon, peeled (1 tablespoon juice)

3½ cups sliced apples, unpeeled

½ teaspoon ground cinnamon

⅔ cup chopped apricots (dried or fresh)

TOPPING

3 cups coarsely chopped unsalted pecans

1 cup coarsely chopped unsalted macadamia nuts

1 cup pure maple syrup

3 tablespoons safflower oil

2 teaspoons pure almond extract

1 teaspoon grated orange peel

2 teaspoons ground cinnamon

¼ cup chopped dates

1 Preheat the oven to 400°F.

2 Separately push the pears, the 2 apples (not the slices), the orange, and the lemon through the juicer. Set aside ½ cup of the pear juice and ¾ cup of the pear pulp, ½ cup of the apple juice and ¾ cup of the apple pulp, ¼ cup of the orange juice, and 1 tablespoon of the lemon juice.

3 In a medium-sized mixing bowl, combine the apple slices with the pear, apple, and orange juices. Stir in the pear and apple pulp, lemon juice, ½ teaspoon of cinnamon, and apricots, mixing well.

4 In another medium-sized mixing bowl, combine all the topping ingredients except the dates and 1 teaspoon of the cinnamon, mixing well.

5 In a small mixing bowl, combine the dates with the remaining 1 teaspoon of cinnamon, and mix well.

6 Pour the apple slice mixture into a greased 9-by-12-inch baking dish, spreading the filling evenly so that it touches all sides of the pan.

7 Pour the topping over the filling, and spread it evenly with a knife.

8 Bake the cobbler for 30–35 minutes, or until the apples are soft. Remove from the oven, and sprinkle with the cinnamon and dates mixture.

9 Serve hot or cold with rice or soy ice cream.

MAKES 6–8 SERVINGS

Sweet Potato Pie

1 apple (¼ cup juice)
3 cups mashed steamed sweet potatoes
vegetarian egg substitute for 2 eggs
¼ cup pure maple syrup
1½ teaspoons ground allspice
1 recipe Basic Spelt Crust, prebaked (see page 171)

1 Preheat the oven to 350°F.

2 Push the apple through the juicer. Set aside ¼ cup of the juice.

3 In a blender or food processor, combine the apple juice, sweet potatoes, egg substitute, maple syrup, and allspice, and blend until smooth.

4 Pour the sweet potato mixture into the prepared pie crust, and bake for 25 minutes, or until the crust is golden and the filling is set.

5 Allow the pie to cool for 10 minutes before serving.

MAKES ONE 9-INCH PIE

Basic Spelt Crust

1 cup whole spelt flour
½ teaspoon ground cinnamon
4 tablespoons extra virgin olive oil
¼ cup plus 3 tablespoons cold water or unsweetened soymilk

1 In a small mixing bowl, combine the whole spelt flour and cinnamon.

2 With a fork or pastry cutter, mix the olive oil into the flour mixture until the mixture is moist and fine. Add the cold water (or soymilk) by the tablespoon until the dough has a smooth, even consistency.

3 Roll the dough into a ball, and place it in a bowl. Cover the bowl with plastic wrap, and chill for 1 hour.

4 Flour a smooth, clean surface and a rolling pin with all-purpose flour. Place the chilled dough on the floured surface, and roll the dough from the center out until it is ½ inch larger than a 9-inch pie plate. (Check by placing the empty pie plate on top of the rolled dough.)

5 Loosen the dough by gently sliding a floured spatula underneath it toward the center, and moving around the entire area of the dough until it can be lifted. Transfer the dough to a lightly greased 9-inch pie plate.

6 When a recipe calls for a baked crust, put the crust in a 350°F oven for 15 minutes, or until light brown in color.

MAKES ONE 9-INCH CRUST

Sweet Potato Crust

4 sweet potatoes, steamed and chilled (2 cups pulp)
vegetarian egg substitute for 1 egg
¼ cup finely chopped dates
½ teaspoon pure almond extract

1 Preheat the oven to 350°F.

2 Push the sweet potatoes through the juicer. Set aside 2 cups of the pulp.

3 In a small mixing bowl, combine the sweet potato pulp, egg substitute, dates, and almond extract, and mix together well.

4 Press the mixture into a lightly greased 9-inch pie plate, and bake for 40 minutes, or until golden brown in color.

MAKES ONE 9-INCH CRUST

Date Nut Crust

3 parsnips (½ cup pulp)
3 cups whole pitted dates
1½ cups unsalted pecans, soaked for 24 hours and drained

1 Push the parsnips through the juicer. Set aside ½ cup of the pulp.

2 In a blender or food processor, combine the parsnip pulp, dates, and pecans, and blend until smooth.

3 Press the mixture into a lightly greased 9-inch pie plate.

4 When a recipe calls for a baked crust, put the crust in a 350°F oven for 15 minutes, or until light brown in color.

MAKES ONE 9-INCH CRUST

A Sunny Day Crust

1 cup unsalted roasted cashews
⅓ cup yellow cornmeal
⅓ cup quinoa flour
⅓ cup unsweetened coconut
a pinch of sea salt
¼ cup extra virgin olive oil
¼ cup freshly squeezed lemon juice
1 teaspoon honey (optional)

1 Preheat the oven to 325°F. Lightly oil and flour a 13-by-4-by-1½-inch tart pan with a removable bottom and set aside.

2 In a food processor, using the metal blade, process the cashews until they are powder-fine. Add the cornmeal, flour, coconut, and salt and process until well combined. Restart the food processor, and slowly add the oil, lemon juice, and honey, if desired, through the feed tube. Process until soft and crumbly.

3 Transfer the mixture to the prepared pan and distribute evenly. Press and shape the dough into the pan to form an even crust.

4 Place the tart pan on top of a cookie sheet and bake in the preheated oven for 25–30 minutes, or until golden. For uniformity in baking, rotate the sheet from front to back halfway through the baking period. Remove the sheet from the oven, transfer to a wire rack, and cool completely.

MAKES 1 CRUST

Banana Almond Bread

1 peeled banana, frozen (½ cup pulp)
vegetarian egg substitute for 1 egg
½ cup light-colored honey (clover, tupelo, or wildflower)
⅓ cup cold-pressed flavorless oil (sunflower or safflower)
1 teaspoon pure almond extract
1¼ cups plus 1 tablespoon whole spelt flour
1 teaspoon baking soda
½ teaspoon ground nutmeg
½ teaspoon ground cinnamon
¼ teaspoon sea salt
½ cup water
¼ cup slivered blanched almonds

1 Preheat the oven to 350°F.

2 Push the frozen banana through the juicer. Set aside ½ cup of the pulp (mashed banana).

3 In a medium-sized mixing bowl, combine the egg substitute, honey, oil, and almond extract.

4 In a small mixing bowl, sift together the flour, baking soda, nutmeg, cinnamon, and salt.

5 Add a small amount of the flour mixture to the egg substitute mixture, and blend well. Then add a small amount of the water to the egg substitute mixture, and blend well. Alternate adding the remaining flour mixture and the water to the egg mixture, making sure to blend well after each addition.

6 Add the banana and almonds to the batter, and mix well with a sturdy spoon.

7 Pour the batter into a greased 3-by-7-inch loaf pan. Bake for 15 minutes, remove the loaf from the oven, and make a 1-inch-deep slice lengthwise down the center of the loaf (this facilitates cooking the center). Return the loaf to the oven, and bake for an additional 25–30 minutes, or until a toothpick inserted in the center comes out clean.

8 Allow the bread to cool for 5 minutes before removing it from the pan. Cool the bread for at least 5 additional minutes before slicing.

MAKES ONE 3-BY-7-INCH LOAF

Gingerbread

1 small piece ginger root (¼ teaspoon juice and ¼ teaspoon pulp)
⅓ cup safflower oil
½ cup light-colored honey (tupelo, clover, or wildflower)
⅓ cup unsulphured blackstrap molasses
vegetarian egg substitute for 1 egg
¼ cup chopped dates
½ cup unsweetened soymilk
¼ cup water
1¾ cups plus 1 tablespoon whole spelt flour
1 teaspoon baking powder
½ teaspoon ground cinnamon
¼ teaspoon ground nutmeg
¼ teaspoon sea salt
1 recipe Cocoa Coconut Frosting (see page 177)

1   Preheat the oven to 350°F.

2   Push the ginger through the juicer. Set aside ¼ teaspoon of the juice and ¼ teaspoon of the pulp.

3   In a medium-sized mixing bowl, combine the ginger juice and pulp, oil, honey, molasses, egg substitute, dates, soymilk, and water. Stir the ingredients well.

4   In a small mixing bowl, sift together the flour, baking powder, cinnamon, nutmeg, and salt. Add to the oil mixture, and blend well.

5 Grease the bottom of a 9-inch round or 10-inch square baking pan, line with parchment paper, and regrease. Pour the batter into the pan, and bake for 15–20 minutes, or until a toothpick inserted in the center of the cake comes out clean.

6 Allow the cake to cool for 5 minutes before removing it from the pan. Remove the parchment paper, and cool completely before glazing with Cocoa Coconut Frosting.

MAKES ONE 9-INCH CAKE

Cocoa Coconut Frosting

¾ cup light-colored honey (clover, tupelo, or wildflower)
¼ cup plus 2 tablespoons pure unsweetened cocoa powder
(unsweetened carob powder may be substituted)
3 tablespoons plain soy yogurt (optional)
1 teaspoon pure almond extract
2 tablespoons unsweetened flaked coconut

1 In a small mixing bowl, whisk together all of the ingredients, except the coconut, until a smooth frosting is formed.

2 Add the coconut, and mix well.

MAKES 1 CUP

mpkin and Spice Muffins

1 sweet potato, steamed and chilled (½ cup juice)
½ small pumpkin (¾ cup pulp)
¾ cup unsalted walnut halves
vegetarian egg substitute for 2 eggs
½ cup plus 2 tablespoons cold-pressed flavorless oil (sunflower,
     safflower)
½ cup chopped dates
1 banana, mashed
1 teaspoon pure vanilla extract
2 cups stone-ground whole spelt flour
1 teaspoon baking powder
1 teaspoon baking soda
1 teaspoon ground nutmeg
½ teaspoon ground allspice
½ teaspoon ground cinnamon
½ cup raisins

1 Preheat the oven to 350°F.

2 Separately push the sweet potato and pumpkin through the juicer. Set aside ½ cup of the sweet potato juice (pumpkin juice may be substituted), and ¾ cup of the pumpkin pulp.

3 In the oven, toast the walnuts on an ungreased cookie sheet for approximately 10 minutes, stirring occasionally. (Be careful not to let them burn, as this causes bitterness.) Coarsely chop the nuts and set aside.

4 In a medium-sized mixing bowl, combine the sweet potato juice, egg substitute, oil, dates, banana, and vanilla extract, and mix well with a sturdy spoon. Add the pumpkin pulp to the mixture, and stir.

5 In a small mixing bowl, sift together the flour, baking powder, baking soda, nutmeg, allspice, and cinnamon.

6 Add the flour mixture to the egg substitute mixture, and blend well. Stir in the toasted nuts and raisins.

7 Pour the batter into greased or paper-lined muffin tins, and bake for 25–30 minutes, or until a toothpick inserted in the center of a muffin comes out clean.

MAKES 24 MUFFINS

t Walnut Cake

2 oranges (½ cup juice)
2 sweet potatoes, steamed and chilled (1 cup juice)
6 carrots (1½ cups pulp)
1½ cups unsalted walnut halves
¾ cup unsalted pecan halves
vegetarian egg substitute for 2 eggs
1 cup cold-pressed safflower flavorless oil
1 cup light-colored honey (clover, tupelo, or wildflower)
2 teaspoons pure almond extract
4½ cups stone-ground whole spelt flour
2¼ teaspoons baking powder
1¼ teaspoons baking soda
1 teaspoon ground cinnamon
½ teaspoon ground nutmeg
¼ teaspoon ground cloves
1 cup chopped dates

1 Preheat the oven to 350°F.

2 Separately push the oranges, sweet potatoes, and carrots through the juicer. Set aside ½ cup of the orange juice, 1 cup of the sweet potato juice (carrot juice may be substituted), and 1½ cups of the carrot pulp.

3 In the oven, toast the walnuts and pecans on an ungreased cookie sheet for approximately 10 minutes, stirring occasionally. (Be careful not to let them burn, as this causes bitterness.) Coarsely chop the nuts and set aside.

4 In a medium-sized mixing bowl, combine the orange and sweet potato juices, egg substitute, oil, honey, and almond extract, and mix well. Stir in the carrot pulp.

5 In a large mixing bowl, sift the flour with the baking powder, baking soda, cinnamon, nutmeg, and cloves.

6 Add the egg substitute mixture to the flour mixture, and blend with an electric hand-held mixer until smooth. Add the dates and toasted nuts to the batter, and mix well.

7 Pour the batter into 2 greased 3-by-7-inch loaf pans, and bake for 45 minutes to 1 hour, or until a toothpick inserted in the center of the loaves comes out clean.

8 Allow the loaves to cool for about 5 minutes before removing from the pans. Cool the loaves for at least 5 additional minutes before slicing.

MAKES TWO 3-BY-7-INCH LOAVES

Raspberry Crowned Lemon Tart

1 3-ounce pkg. custard mix (any type without eggs or dairy)
juice of 2 lemons (freshly squeezed)
4 tablespoons honey
1 recipe prebaked A Sunny Day Crust (see page 173)
1 pint fresh raspberries
1 recipe Smooth Vanilla Sauce (see page 210)
1 recipe Red Raspberry Coulis (see page 211)

1 Prepare custard as directed on package. Combine custard, lemon juice, and honey. Mix well.

2 To assemble the tart, pour the honey lemon custard into the baked tart shell and spread evenly. Then carefully distribute the berries on top.

3 Refrigerate for 60 minutes or until well set and firm to the touch. Carefully push up the bottom and slide the tart off of the disc and onto a cutting board.

sing a sharp knife, slice into 10–12 equal wedges and serve
n dessert plates accompanied by a drizzling of Smooth
Vanilla Sauce and Red Raspberry Coulis.

MAKES 1 PIE

Almond Butter Cookies

2–3 parsnips (⅓ cup pulp)
¼ cup almonds
4 tablespoons safflower oil
⅓ cup light-colored honey (clover, tupelo, or wildflower)
2 teaspoons pure almond extract
3 cups spelt flour
2 tablespoons baking powder
1 teaspoon sea salt
1½ teaspoons ground cinnamon
½ cup ground unsalted almonds or almond butter
¼ cup chopped dates

1 Push the parsnips through the juicer. Set aside ⅓ cup of the
   pulp.

2 In the oven, toast the almonds on an ungreased cookie sheet
   for approximately 10 minutes at 350°F, stirring occasionally.
   (Be careful not to let them burn, as this causes bitterness.) In a
   blender, food processor, or food mill, grind the nuts and set
   aside.

3 In a medium-sized mixing bowl, cream together the oil,
   honey, and almond extract.

4 In another medium-sized mixing bowl, sift together the flour,
   baking powder, salt, and 1 teaspoon of the cinnamon.

5 Add the flour mixture to the oil mixture, and stir to blend. Stir in the ½ cup ground almonds (or almond butter) and the parsnip pulp, blending thoroughly with a sturdy spoon.

6 Roll the dough into a log, and cover with plastic wrap. Chill for 1 hour.

7 Preheat the oven to 350°F.

8 In a small mixing bowl, combine the remaining ½ teaspoon of cinnamon with the dates and the ground toasted almonds.

9 Remove the cookie dough from the refrigerator. On a floured surface, roll the dough to ¼-inch thickness with a rolling pin, and use cookie cutters to cut the dough into the desired shapes. Sprinkle the shapes with the cinnamon mixture, and bake on an ungreased cookie sheet for 10–15 minutes, or until the cookies are light brown along the edges.

MAKES 18 COOKIES

Holiday Surprise Cookies

2 sweet potatoes, steamed and chilled (1 cup pulp)

1 cup unsalted pecan halves

1 cup unsalted walnut halves

vegetarian substitute for 2 eggs

1½ cups chopped dates

2 tablespoons pure maple syrup

½ cup safflower oil

1 teaspoon pure vanilla extract

1 teaspoon pure almond extract

1⅔ cups plus 2 tablespoons whole spelt flour

1 teaspoon baking soda

1 teaspoon baking powder

1 teaspoon ground cinnamon

½ teaspoon sea salt

1½ cups raisins

1 cup rolled oats

½ cup unsweetened carob chips

¼ cup unsweetened flaked coconut

¼ cup unsalted hulled sunflower seeds

1   Preheat the oven to 375°F.

2   Push the sweet potatoes through the juicer. Set aside 1 cup of the pulp.

3   In the oven, toast the pecans and walnuts on an ungreased cookie sheet for approximately 10 minutes, stirring occasionally. (Be careful not to let them burn, as this causes bitterness.) Coarsely chop the nuts and set aside.

4 In a medium-sized mixing bowl, combine the sweet potato pulp, egg substitute, dates, maple syrup, safflower oil, and vanilla and almond extracts. Blend well with an electric hand-held mixer.

5 In a small mixing bowl, sift together the flour, baking soda, baking powder, cinnamon, and salt.

6 Add the flour mixture to the sweet potato mixture, and blend well with a sturdy spoon. Stir in the toasted nuts, raisins, oats, carob chips, coconut, and sunflower seeds, and mix well.

7 Roll the dough into ¼-inch balls. Place the balls on an un-greased cookie sheet, and bake for 15 minutes, or until the cookies turn light brown in color.

MAKES 30 COOKIES

Fruit and Nut Cookies

1 carrot (⅛ cup pulp)
½ cup unsalted pecan halves
¾ cup whole unsalted almonds
vegetarian egg substitute for 1 egg
3 tablespoons safflower oil
1 cup chopped dates
2 tablespoons pure maple syrup
¼ teaspoon pure vanilla extract
½ teaspoon pure almond extract
¾ cup whole spelt flour
½ teaspoon baking soda
⅛ teaspoon sea salt
½ cup unsweetened carob chips
¼ cup rolled oats
½ cup raisins

1 Preheat the oven to 375°F.

2 Push the carrot through the juicer. Set aside ⅛ cup of the pulp.

3 In the oven, toast the pecans and almonds on an ungreased cookie sheet for approximately 10 minutes, stirring occasionally. (Be careful not to let them burn, as this causes bitterness.) Coarsely chop the nuts and set aside.

4 In a medium-sized mixing bowl, cream together the egg substitute, oil, dates, maple syrup, and vanilla and almond extracts. Add the carrot pulp, and mix well.

5 In a small mixing bowl, sift together the flour, baking soda, and salt.

6 Add the flour mixture to the carrot mixture, and blend well with a sturdy spoon. Stir in the nuts, carob chips, oats, and raisins.

7 Roll the dough into ¼-inch balls. Place the balls on an ungreased cookie sheet, and bake for 15 minutes, or until the cookies are golden brown in color.

MAKES 18 COOKIES

Living Protein Squares

MEDJOOL DATE BOTTOM
1 cup sunflower seeds
1 cup medjool dates, pitted
1 cup peanut butter
1 banana, peeled and halved
1 teaspoon pure vanilla flavor
¼ cup sifted carob powder
1 cup flaxseed meal
1 cup green vegetable powder
1 cup unsweetened coconut

HONEY PEANUT TOPPING
1½ cups peanut butter
2 tablespoons honey

1 To prepare the Medjool Date Bottom, in a food processor, using the metal blade, process the sunflower seeds until powder-fine. Add the dates, peanut butter, banana, and vanilla. Process until well blended, about 2 minutes. Restart the food processor, and add the carob powder, flaxseed meal, green powder, and coconut through the feed tube. Run until well combined, about 10 seconds.

2 With your hands, shape the date mixture into 1-inch squares (oil your hands slightly to prevent sticking). Set the squares onto a cookie sheet lined with parchment paper and set aside.

3 To prepare the honey peanut topping, in a food processor, using the metal blade, process the peanut butter and honey until well blended.

4 With a knife, dot each square with a peanut honey top. Transfer the cookie sheet to the refrigerator and chill the squares on the top shelf for 1–2 hours or until firm.

5 Serve accompanied by a cup of herbal tea.

MAKES 8 SERVINGS

Fudge Brownies

snips (½ cup pulp)
1 cup whole spelt flour
1 teaspoon baking powder
½ cup safflower oil
vegetarian egg substitute for 1 egg
¼ cup pure maple syrup
1 cup pure unsweetened cocoa powder (unsweetened carob powder
   may be substituted)
2½ cups chopped dates
1 teaspoon pure vanilla extract
½ cup ground unsalted almonds or almond butter
1 cup coarsely chopped unsalted walnuts

1 Preheat the oven to 350°F.

2 Push the parsnips through the juicer. Set aside ½ cup of the pulp.

3 In a small mixing bowl, sift together the flour and baking powder.

4 In a large mixing bowl, combine the oil, egg substitute, maple syrup, and cocoa. Add the parsnip pulp, dates, and vanilla extract, and mix well. Add the flour mixture, and mix again. Stir in the almonds and walnuts.

5 Pour the batter into a greased 10-inch square pan, and bake for 30–40 minutes, or until firm.

6 Allow to cool slightly before cutting into 12 squares.

MAKES 12 BROWNIES

Pecan Chewies

6 parsnips (1 cup pulp)
1½ cups sweet rice syrup
½ cup raw almond butter
3 teaspoons pure almond extract
2 cups coarsely chopped unsalted pecans
1 cup blanched slivered almonds

1 Preheat the oven to 350°F.

2 Push the parsnips through the juicer. Set aside 1 cup of the pulp.

3 In a medium-sized mixing bowl, combine the sweet rice syrup, almond butter, and almond extract. Add the parsnip pulp, pecans, and almonds, and mix well.

4 Pour the mixture into a greased 9-inch square baking dish, and bake for 10 minutes, or until the nuts begin to turn light brown in color.

5 Cool for about 5 minutes before cutting into 6 squares.

MAKES 6 CHEWIES

Carob Power Brownies

½ cup sunflower seeds
1½ cups brown rice flour
½ cup carob powder
¾ teaspoon baking powder
¾ teaspoon ground nutmeg
¾ teaspoon sea salt
½ cup extra virgin olive oil
5 large bananas, peeled and coarsely chopped (about 2¼ cups)
1 cup bottled apple juice
1 cup bottled apricot juice
1 tablespoon honey
1½ teaspoons pure banana flavor
1 cup walnuts, coarsely chopped
1 cup oat bran
½ cup + 2 tablespoons rice bran
½ cup dairy-free carob chips

1 Preheat oven to 350°F. Line two 12-well muffin tins with paper baking cups and set aside.

2 Using a mini food processor or coffee grinder, process the sunflower seeds until powder-fine. Transfer to a mixing bowl and set aside.

3 To make the brownies, in a large mixing bowl, sift together the flour, carob powder, baking powder, nutmeg, and salt. Whisk together until well mixed. Set aside.

4 In a food processor, using a metal blade, combine the oil and banana. Process until creamy, about 1 minute. Pour in the

apple juice, apricot juice, honey, and banana flavor. Process until well blended.

5 With a rubber spatula, gradually add the wet ingredients to the dry, making sure they are well blended before each addition. Scrape off any excess batter from the side of the bowl. Stir in the walnuts, oat bran, rice bran, and chips until well mixed. Spoon the batter into the prepared muffin tins (the wells will be half full).

6 Bake in the middle level of the preheated oven for 35–40 minutes. For uniformity in baking, rotate the tin from front to back halfway through the baking period.

7 The brownies are done when a tester inserted in the center comes out clean. Remove the brownies from the oven and let cool completely, about 15–20 minutes.

8 Serve with a glass of rice milk, soymilk, or nut milk.

MAKES 24 BROWNIES

Carob Fruit Bars

4 carrots (1 cup pulp)
¾ cup pure maple syrup
vegetarian egg substitute for 2 eggs
¼ cup light-colored honey (clover, tupelo, or wildflower)
1 teaspoon pure almond extract
½ teaspoon ground cinnamon
1 cup mashed banana
1 cup unsweetened flaked coconut
¾ cup unsweetened carob chips
1 cup coarsely chopped unsalted pecans
*¼ cup coarsely chopped unsalted macadamia nuts (pecans may be
    substituted)*
2 tablespoons light oil
½ cup whole spelt flour

1. Preheat the oven to 375°F.

2. Push the carrots through the juicer. Set aside 1 cup of the pulp.

3. In a medium-sized mixing bowl, whisk together the maple syrup, egg substitute, honey, almond extract, and cinnamon. Add the carrot pulp, banana, coconut, carob chips, pecans, and macadamia nuts, and stir well.

4. In another medium-sized mixing bowl, combine the oil and flour, and blend until a dough forms.

5. Press the dough into a greased 9-by-12-inch baking dish. Pour the maple syrup mixture over the crust, and bake for 15–20 minutes.

6. Allow to cool for 10 minutes before slicing into 12 bars.

MAKES 12 BARS

Grain Crispies Treats

1 parsnip (¼ cup pulp)
½ cup plus 2 tablespoons sweet rice syrup
¼ cup peanut butter
1½ teaspoons pure almond extract
3 cups unsweetened grain flake cereal
¼ cup chopped dates

1 Push the parsnip through the juicer. Set aside ¼ cup of the pulp.

2 In a 2-quart saucepan, combine the rice syrup, peanut butter, and almond extract, and bring to a simmer.

3 Remove the mixture from the heat, and stir in the parsnip pulp, grain flakes, and dates, mixing together well.

4 Spoon the mixture into a greased 9-by-12-inch baking dish, and press down firmly.

5 Cool completely before slicing into 9 bars.

MAKES 9 BARS

...ana Cocoa Sundae

2 peeled bananas, frozen (1 cup pulp)
2 tablespoons pure unsweetened cocoa powder (unsweetened carob
  powder may be substituted)
2 tablespoons unsweetened flaked coconut

1. Juice the frozen bananas, and collect 1 cup of the pulp (mashed banana) in a small mixing bowl.

2. Add the cocoa to the pulp, and mix together well.

3. Divide the mixture into two serving dishes, top with the coconut, and serve cold.

MAKES 2 SUNDAES

Banana Nutmeg Sundae with Pineapple and Coconut

2 peeled bananas, frozen (1 cup pulp)
¼ cup fresh pineapple chunks
2 tablespoons unsweetened flaked coconut
¼ teaspoon ground nutmeg

1. Push the frozen bananas through the juicer, and collect 1 cup of the pulp (mashed banana).

2. Divide the banana pulp into two serving dishes, top with the remaining ingredients, and serve cold.

MAKES 2 SUNDAES

Wonder Juice Float

1 medium kiwi, peeled and quartered
1 medium tangerine, peeled and quartered
2 medium oranges, peeled and quartered
¼ medium pineapple, peeled, cored, and cubed
2 ounces sparkling water
1 scoop soy ice cream (approx. ½ cup)

1 Push all the fruits through the juicer.

2 Add the sparkling water to the juice mixture, and stir well.

3 Gently drop scoop of soy ice cream into the juice mixture.

4 Serve immediately.

MAKES 2 CUPS

Strawberry Chocolate Pops

2 peeled bananas, frozen (1 cup pulp)
4 cups honeydew melon chunks, peeled (1⅓ cups juice)
1 cup frozen strawberries
1 tablespoon pure unsweetened cocoa powder (unsweetened carob
*   powder may be substituted)*
1 teaspoon pure lemon extract

1   Separately push the frozen bananas and the melon through
    the juicer. Set aside 1 cup of the banana pulp (mashed
    banana) and 1⅓ cups of the melon juice.

2   In a blender or food processor, combine the banana pulp and
    melon juice with the remaining ingredients, and blend for 2
    minutes, or until smooth.

3   Pour the mixture into six 5-ounce ice-pop molds, and freeze
    for 3–4 hours, or until firm.

MAKES 6 POPS

Creamsicle Pops

8 oranges (2 cups juice)
1 cup plain soy yogurt
¼ cup unsweetened flaked coconut
¼ cup ground unsalted almonds or almond butter
1 tablespoon pure vanilla extract

1   Push the oranges through the juicer. Set aside 2 cups of the
    juice.

2 In a blender or food processor, combine the juice with the remaining ingredients, and blend for 2 minutes, or until smooth.

3 Pour the mixture into six 5-ounce ice-pop molds, and freeze for 3–4 hours, or until firm.

MAKES 6 POPS

Chocolate Coconut Pops

2 peeled bananas, frozen (1 cup pulp)
6 oranges (1½ cups juice)
½ cup plain soy yogurt
¼ cup unsweetened flaked coconut
2 tablespoons pure unsweetened cocoa powder (unsweetened carob
   powder may be substituted)
2 tablespoons ground unsalted pecans or pecan butter
2 teaspoons pure almond extract

1 Separately push the frozen bananas and the oranges through the juicer. Set aside 1 cup of the banana pulp (mashed banana) and 1½ cups of the orange juice.

2 In a blender or food processor, combine the banana pulp and orange juice with the remaining ingredients, and blend for two minutes, or until smooth.

3 Pour the mixture into six 5-ounce ice-pop molds, and freeze for 3–4 hours, or until firm.

MAKES 6 POPS

Raspberry Melon Pops

4 cups peeled watermelon chunks (1⅓ cups juice)
2 cups peeled honeydew melon chunks (⅔ cup juice)
2 lemons (¼ cup juice)
1½ cups frozen raspberries
2 teaspoons lemon extract

1 Separately push the watermelon, honeydew melon, and lemons through the juicer. Set aside 1⅓ cups of the watermelon juice, ⅔ cup of the honeydew melon juice, and ¼ cup of the lemon juice.

2 In a blender or food processor, combine the juices with the remaining ingredients, and blend for 2 minutes, or until smooth.

3 Pour the mixture into six 5-ounce ice-pop molds, and freeze for 3–4 hours, or until firm.

MAKES 6 POPS

Kiwi Lime Pops

6 kiwis (1½ cups juice)
4 cups peeled honeydew melon chunks (1⅓ cups juice)
2 lemons (3 tablespoons juice)
2 limes (3 tablespoons juice)

1 Separately push the kiwis, melon, lemons, and limes through the juicer. Set aside 1½ cups of the kiwi juice, 1⅓ cups of the melon juice, 3 tablespoons of the lemon juice, and 3 tablespoons of the lime juice.

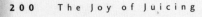

2 In a small mixing bowl, combine the juices, mixing well with a spoon.

3 Pour the mixture into six 5-ounce ice-pop molds, and freeze for 3–4 hours, or until firm.

MAKES 6 POPS

Tropical Pops

6 apples (1½ cups juice)
3 carrots (⅔ cup juice)
2 peeled bananas, frozen (1 cup pulp)
3 tablespoons chopped dates
3 tablespoons unsweetened flaked coconut
3 tablespoons ground unsalted almonds or almond butter
1 teaspoon ground nutmeg
1 teaspoon pure almond extract

1 Separately push the apples, carrots, and frozen bananas through the juicer. Set aside 1½ cups of the apple juice, ⅔ cup of the carrot juice, and 1 cup of the banana pulp (mashed banana).

2 In a blender or food processor, combine the juices and pulp with the remaining ingredients, and blend for 2 minutes, or until smooth.

3 Pour the mixture into six 5-ounce ice-pop molds, and freeze for 3–4 hours, or until firm.

MAKES 6 POPS

Cherry Fruit Pops

1 lemon (2 tablespoons juice)
3 cups frozen pitted cherries (or any frozen berries)

1 Push the lemons through the juicer. Set aside 2 tablespoons of the juice.

2 In a blender or food processor, combine the lemon juice and cherries, and blend for 2 minutes, or until smooth.

3 Pour the mixture into six 5-ounce ice-pop molds, and freeze for 3–4 hours, or until firm.

MAKES 6 POPS

Mango Fruit Pops

4 mangoes (2 cups juice)
1½ pineapples (1½ cups juice)
1½ lemons (3 tablespoons juice)

1 Separately push the mangoes, pineapples, and lemons through the juicer. Set aside 2 cups of the mango juice, 1½ cups of the pineapple juice, and 3 tablespoons of the lemon juice.

2 In a small mixing bowl, combine the juices, mixing well with a spoon.

3 Pour the mixture into six 5-ounce ice-pop molds, and freeze for 3–4 hours, or until firm.

MAKES 6 POPS

Lemon Lime Slush

1 eight-pound honeydew melon, peeled, seeded, and cut into 1-inch
  pieces
8 lemons, peeled
8 limes, peeled
1 large lime, sliced into ¼-inch-thick half-moons, as garnish
  (optional)

1 Place a 4-cup-capacity liquid measuring cup under the juicer
spout. Push the honeydew melon, lemons, and limes through
the juicer. Reserve 1¼ cups juice and set aside in the refrigerator.

2 Pour the remaining juice into 4 ice cube trays and freeze for
1–2 hours or until frozen.

3 Transfer the frozen cubes to a blender or food processor and
blend with the refrigerated juice until slush-like in consistency.

4 Serve in tall glasses with straws and lime slices, if desired.

MAKES 10 CUPS

Pineapple Orange Slush

4 large grapefruits, peeled
4 large oranges, peeled
½ large pineapple, peeled, cored, and cut into 1-inch pieces
   (about 4 cups)
16 nectarines, pitted and quartered

1 Place a 4-cup-capacity liquid measuring cup under the juicer spout. Push the grapefruits, oranges, pineapple, and nectarines through the juicer. Reserve 1¼ cups juice and set aside in the refrigerator.

2 Pour the remaining juice into 4 ice cube trays and freeze for 1–2 hours or until frozen.

3 Transfer the frozen cubes to a blender or food processor and blend with the refrigerated juice until slush-like in consistency.

4 Serve in tall glasses with straws.

MAKES 12 CUPS

The "Sublime" Water Slush

1 eight-pound watermelon, peeled and cut into 1-inch cubes
3 large limes, peeled
1 lime, sliced into ¼-inch-thick half-moons, as garnish (optional)

1 Place a 4-cup-capacity liquid measuring cup under the juicer spout. Push the watermelon and 3 limes through the juicer. Reserve 1¼ cups juice and set aside in the refrigerator.

2 Pour the remaining juice into 4 ice cube trays and freeze for 1–2 hours or until frozen.

3 Transfer the frozen cubes to a blender or food processor and blend with the refrigerated juice until slush-like in consistency.

4 Serve in tall glasses with straws and lime slices, if desired.

MAKES 9–10 CUPS

Tropical Ambrosia Pudding

1 tangerine (¼ cup juice)
1 mango (½ cup juice)
¼ pineapple (¼ cup juice)
1½ cups silken tofu
¼ cup pure maple syrup
2 teaspoons pure almond extract
¼ teaspoon ground nutmeg
¾ cup mashed banana
3 tablespoons unsweetened flaked coconut
3 tablespoons raisins
3 tablespoons blanched slivered almonds

1 Separately push the tangerine, mango, and pineapple through the juicer. Set aside ¼ cup of the tangerine juice, ½ cup of the mango juice, and ¼ cup of the pineapple juice.

2 In a blender or food processor, combine the juices with the silken tofu, and blend for 2–3 minutes, or until smooth.

3 Add the maple syrup, almond extract, and nutmeg, and continue to blend.

4 Transfer the mixture to a small mixing bowl, and stir in the banana, coconut, raisins, and almonds.

5 Chill for at least 1 hour before serving.

MAKES 2–4 SERVINGS

Applesauce

5 apples (1¼ cups juice and 1 cup pulp)
1 tablespoon raisins
dash of ground cinnamon

1 Push the apples through the juicer. Set aside 1¼ cups of the juice and 1 cup of the pulp.

2 In a small saucepan, bring the apple juice to a boil over high heat.

3 Reduce the heat to medium-low, and add the apple pulp, raisins, and cinnamon. Simmer for 5–10 minutes.

4 Serve hot or cold.

MAKES 1½ CUPS

Strawberry Compote with Saffron Flowers

¼ pineapple (¼ cup juice)
1 teaspoon saffron threads
1 cup sliced strawberries
1 cup mashed banana
¼ teaspoon ground nutmeg

1 Push the pineapple through the juicer. Set aside ¼ cup of the juice.

2 In a small saucepan, combine the pineapple juice with the saffron threads. Cook over medium heat until the mixture comes to a simmer, and remove from the heat.

3. In a blender or food processor, combine the pineapple mixture with the remaining ingredients, and blend for two minutes, or until smooth. Transfer to a small bowl, and chill for 1 hour.

4. Serve cold over cake or ice cream.

MAKES 2 CUPS

Granola Delight

1 cup granola
1 cup rice beverage
½ cup unsweetened carob chips
1 cup vanilla soy ice cream
2 bananas, peeled
2 cups strawberries, hulled
raspberry syrup

1. Blend all the ingredients together in a blender until well combined.

2. Transfer blended mixture to dishes and drizzle desired amount of raspberry syrup over the top.

3. Serve immediately.

MAKES 5 CUPS

Almond Joy with Soy

4 ounces purified water
20 unsalted almonds
2 dates, pitted
2 ounces soft tofu

1 Blend all the ingredients together in a blender until smooth.

2 Serve immediately.

MAKES 1 CUP

Cherry Grape Kanten

6 cups bottled pineapple juice
¼ cup + 2 tablespoons agar flakes (available at healthfood stores)
2 tablespoons freshly squeezed lemon juice
8 medium ripe peaches, peeled, pitted, and sliced (about 3 cups)
¼ large pineapple, peeled, cored, and cut into 1-inch pieces (about 2 cups)
2 cups seedless green grapes
2 twelve-ounce packages frozen pitted cherries

1 In a medium-sized saucepan, bring the pineapple juice to a boil over high heat. Reduce heat to moderate and stir in the agar.

2 Simmer uncovered, stirring occasionally, for 10 minutes or until the agar is completely dissolved.

3 In a large mixing bowl, toss the peaches, pineapple, grapes, and cherries together with the lemon juice until well combined. Transfer to a 7-by-11-inch baking dish and pour in the pineapple juice mixture. Let cool for 15 minutes; then refrigerate for 30–45 minutes or until congealed.

4 Spoon into small bowls and serve.

MAKES 6–8 SERVINGS

Healthy Fondue

2 peeled bananas, frozen
½ cup agar-agar
½ cup carob flavored rice frozen dessert
1 pear, peeled, cored, and quartered
2½ cups pitted cherries
2 teaspoons vanilla powder

1 Blend the bananas, agar-agar, and rice frozen dessert in a blender or food processor until smooth.

2 Push the cherries and pears through the juicer.

3 Add juice mixture and vanilla powder to blended mixture, and blend until well combined.

4 Transfer mixture to a small pot and heat over low heat until warm. Use as a fondue dip for a variety of diced fruit or vegetables. In the alternative, freeze blended mixture and serve frozen in a bowl.

MAKES 3 CUPS

herry Yogurt Sauce

1 cup pitted cherries (½ cup juice and ½ cup pulp)
1 cup plain soy yogurt

1 Push the cherries through the juicer. Set aside ½ cup of the juice and ½ cup of the pulp.

2 In a small mixing bowl, combine the juice, pulp, and yogurt, and stir until the mixture is well blended.

3 Serve cold with sliced fresh fruit, or spoon over cake.

Variations: Substitute strawberries, blueberries, or raspberries for the cherries.

MAKES 2 CUPS

Smooth Vanilla Sauce

2 cups vanilla-flavored soymilk
1 cup lite coconut milk
1 vanilla bean, cut in half lengthwise (about 3.5 grams)
2 teaspoons honey
¼ teaspoon sea salt
1 teaspoon pure vanilla flavor

1 In a medium-sized saucepan, bring the soymilk and coconut milk to a simmer. With a wooden spoon, stir in the vanilla bean, honey, and salt. Reduce heat to low and simmer uncovered, stirring occasionally for 25–30 minutes, or until the sauce reduces by two-thirds. Remove from the heat then stir in the vanilla flavor until well combined.

2 Serve hot or chilled over fresh fruit.

MAKES 3 CUPS

Red Raspberry Coulis

2 cups frozen red raspberries
½ cup frozen orange juice concentrate

1 In a food processor, using the metal blade, combine the raspberries and concentrate. Process until creamy about 3 minutes. Remove the blade, and use a rubber spatula to scrape off any excess coulis remaining on the blade or processor.

2 Serve immediately.

MAKES 2½ CUPS

Gary Null's Natural-Living Weight-Loss Tips

1. *Stop* being a couch potato.

   Start being more active.

   Exert more energy—use the stairs more, walk farther and for longer periods of time, and participate in more sports. Gradually establish a regular exercise routine involving running, cycling, or another aerobic activty.

2. *Stop* procrastinating.

   Start getting things done.

   Finishing things that you have been putting off will make you feel better about yourself and help keep your mind off food. Take up a cause, hobby, project, or even a new romance that renews your interest in life and makes you want to get up in the morning.

3. *Stop* being passive.

   Start taking charge of your life.

   Using food for comfort and reward is inappropriate, and soothing your sorrows and frustrations with fattening foods may actually deepen your depression. Instead of overeating, analyze what is bothering you, and take steps to eliminate the problem.

4. *Stop* punishing yourself with food.

Start accepting yourself for what you are.

Food is generally thought of as being pleasurable, but you might subconsciously be using food to punish yourself. Secretly, you may believe that you don't deserve to be pretty, popular, happy, or healthy. Stop being so hard on yourself, and start loving who you really are.

5. *Stop* setting idealistic long-term goals that are difficult to achieve.

Start setting realistic short-term goals that you can reach.

Whether the long-term goal is losing 10 pounds in one month or losing 100 pounds in one year, you are sure to run into temporary plateaus and disappointments—disappointments that could discourage you from continuing your efforts. It is better to set goals day by day or week by week. Then, if you make a mistake, you can forget it and move on to the next goal.

6. *Stop* isolating yourself.

Start seeing people.

Seeing people will help get your mind off food and end the depressing isolation you may impose on yourself when you feel fat and unattractive. Don't think you have to go it alone. If necessary, get help from a counselor or support group.

7. *Stop* thinking of yourself as dieting, starving, or deprived.

Start realizing that you are permanently changing your life for the better.

Generally, diets do not work. Most people regain lost weight in a dangerous diet yo-yo syndrome. Accept the fact that the healthy dietary changes you are making are permanent.

8. *Stop* putting food at the center of your life.

Start expanding your life in new areas.

Minimize the role of food in your social life. Join friends for sports or a movie rather than lunch. Find pleasurable activities other than meals to share with your family.

9. *Stop* thinking that you have to eat when and what the people around you are eating.

Start eating only when you should eat and only what is good for you.

If the three square meals a day your family eats are causing you unnecessary weight gain, don't eat them, *even if it means not eating with or cooking for your family.* You may need six small snacks a day to avoid the hunger pangs that sometimes plague meal-stretched stomachs.

10. *Stop* eating fats, animal products, and "empty calories" (sugar, refined carbohydrates, alcohol, etc.).

Start eating more vegetables, fruits, and whole grains.

Losing weight has less to do with counting calories than with eating right. Vegetables, fruits, and whole grains not only help you lose weight, but also make you healthier because of their high vitamin, mineral, and fiber contents.

Vegetarian's Vocabulary

Arugula. A dark green, somewhat bitter lettuce, commonly used in salads.

Barley. A grain that, while lower in fiber than other grains, is one of the easiest to digest. In a process called "pearling," barley's tough outer hull, which is almost impossible to digest, is removed.

Basil. An herb with bright green, pungent leaves. Basil is commonly used in Italian dishes.

Basmati rice. A variety of Indian-grown rice with a distinctive nutty flavor and a light, fluffy texture.

Blackstrap molasses. A rich, deep-brown sweetener that is the by-product of the process through which sugar cane is converted into refined sugar. Blackstrap molasses contains 35 percent sucrose, and is a good source of iron, calcium, and the B vitamins.

Buckwheat flour. A dark, finely ground, highly nutritious flour made from the seeds of a plant native to Asia.

Bulghur wheat. A grain made from whole wheat that has been cracked, parboiled, and dried. Because of the parboiling, bulghur wheat can be prepared quickly.

Canola oil. The mild-flavored oil extracted from the rapeseed.

Cardamom. An aromatic spice made by grinding the small, dark pods of a tropical plant native to Asia.

Carob. A rich-tasting dark brown powder made from the dried pods of a Mediterranean evergreen tree. Naturally sweet, carob powder can be used as is, or in the form of carob chips, and is a healthful alternative to chocolate.

Celery seeds. Small, light brown, aromatic seeds that come from the wild celery plant.

Cilantro. The pungent, parsley-like leaves of the coriander plant.

Cocoa powder. A powder made by roasting and grinding cacao seeds, and removing most of their oil.

Coriander. A spice made from the dried ripe seeds of the coriander plant. Coriander is commonly used in Asian dishes.

Cream of brown rice. A whole-grain cereal that must be cooked before eating. Cream of brown rice can be purchased in health-food scores.

Date sugar. A natural sweetener made of dehydrated ground dates.

Extract. A concentrated flavoring made by combining alcohol with the oil extracted from almonds, lemons, vanilla, etc.

Garbanzo beans (chickpeas). A bean originally cultivated in the Middle East, where it is still considered a staple food item. Garbanzo beans—also called chickpeas and ceci—are used to make hummus, falafel, meatless loaves, dressings, and breads. They are also a popular addition to salads.

Kasha. Toasted buckwheat, also called buckwheat groats.

Lentils. Tasty beans that are a good source of protein, vitamin A, thiamin, riboflavin, niacin, iron, calcium, phosphorus, and potassium.

Maple syrup. A natural sweetener with a rich flavor made by collecting and boiling the sap of maple trees until the sap becomes thick and sweet.

Millet. A light, fluffy, mild-tasting grain that is high in protein and well tolerated by people who are allergic to other grains. Only hulled millet is suitable for cooking.

Miso. A savory paste made from fermented soybeans. Miso is used mainly as a base for soups and sauces.

Nut butter. A spread made by grinding raw or roasted nuts until the nuts have a creamy, spreadable consistency. While the best-known variety is peanut butter, nut butter can be made with any type of nut, including almonds, pecans, and walnuts.

Pine nuts. The edible seeds from certain pines. Also known as pignola and Indian nuts, these small, tasty nuts are low in protein and high in calories. Pine nuts are sometimes used as a vegetable or dessert garnish, and can also be used in the making of pesto.

Protein powder. A dietary supplement commonly consisting of rice, sesame seeds, egg whites, and soy blends. Protein powder is high in protein, complex carbohydrates, and fiber, and is rich in essential vitamins and minerals.

Quinoa. Quick-cooking grain with a delicious, mild flavor. Quinoa is higher in protein, calcium, and iron than any other grain.

Radicchio. A red-colored, strong-flavored lettuce-like vegetable that is frequently used in salads.

Rice syrup. A thick sweetener made from rice, sometimes with the addition of barley malt. Rice syrup is available in Asian food markets and most healthfood stores.

Safflower oil. The oil extracted from the safflower plant, which belongs to the sunflower family. Probably the lightest and least flavorful of the cooking oils, safflower oil is 94 percent unsaturated.

Saffron threads. The dried stigmas of the plant *Crocus sativus*. Saffron is used as a food coloring and a cooking spice.

Sea salt. The salt obtained from evaporated sea water (either from sun or kiln baking). Sea salt is high in trace vitamins and minerals, and contains no chemical additives.

Sesame oil. The oil extracted from sesame seeds. The dark variety, obtained from seeds that were roasted before pressing, has a smoky flavor. The light variety, obtained from unroasted seeds, has a milder flavor. Hot sesame oil contains red pepper. Sesame oil is 87 percent unsaturated.

Sesame seeds. Obtained from the sesame plant, these seeds are an excellent source of protein, unsaturated fatty acids, calcium, magnesium, niacin, and vitamins A and E.

Shiitake mushrooms. Primarily grown in a special area of Japan, these mushrooms are used to flavor soup stocks and vegetable dishes.

Silken tofu. A soft, creamy variety of tofu.

Soymilk. A non-dairy milk made from soybean mash. Soymilk contains no cholesterol.

Spelt. An ancient grain related to wheat. Widely available.

Sprouts. Seeds that have begun to germinate. Sprouts are an excellent source of protein, and contain high levels of vitamins A, B, and E. Common sprouts include alfalfa, lentil, mung bean, and sunflower.

Sunflower oil. The oil extracted from the seeds of the sunflower. Although similar in taste to safflower oil, sunflower oil is slightly stronger in flavor. This oil is 92 percent unsaturated.

Sunflower seeds. The edible seeds of the sunflower. These seeds are a rich source of protein, unsaturated fatty acids, phosphorus, calcium, iron, fluorine, iodine, potassium, magnesium, and zinc. Vitamin D and E and some of the B vitamins are also found in sunflower seeds.

Sweet rich vinegar. A traditional Japanese vinegar made from fermented rice.

Tahini. A paste made by grinding hulled, unroasted sesame seeds. Tahini is high in fat, protein, and calcium.

Tamari. Naturally fermented soy sauce. Tamari is a by-product of traditional miso-making. Easy to digest, tamari contains B vitamins, riboflavin, and niacin.

Tempeh. A fermented soybean product. Tempeh is high in protein, and is the richest vegetable source of vitamin B_{12}.

Tofu. A white, cheeselike product made from soybean curds. Mild-tasting tofu is high in protein, low in fat and calories, and rich in calcium.

Turmeric. A yellow-orange aromatic spice used in many Asian dishes.

Wheat germ. The central base of the wheat kernel. Wheat germ is a rich source of both vitamin E and the B vitamins.

Index

After the Flu Is Gone, 51
agar-agar, 53, 108, 208, 209
alfalfa sprouts, 9, 14, 17, 44, 118
allspice, 61, 145, 146, 170, 178
almond butter, 58, 68, 69, 72, 182, 190,
    191, 198, 201
Almond Butter Cookies, 182–83
almond extract, 127, 168, 172, 174, 177,
    180, 182, 184, 186, 194, 195, 199,
    201, 205
Almond Joy with Soy, 208
almonds, 77, 84, 87, 88, 119, 156, 174, 182,
    186, 190, 191, 198, 201, 205
aloe vera, 8, 33, 35, 44, 53, 56, 59, 60, 66
amaranth, 71
amino acids, 61
Antioxidant Punch, 52
Antioxidant Supreme, 8
antioxidants, 22, 76
Apple Pear Gingerale, 8
Apple Pecan Cobbler, 168–69
Apple Sprouts, 9
apples, 10, 13, 14, 17, 18, 20, 23–25,
    27–30, 33, 36–38, 40–42, 44, 45,
    49–51, 55, 56, 60–66, 68, 71, 74, 76,
    82, 85, 86, 88–90, 111, 127, 146, 170,
    192, 201

Applesauce, 206
apricots, 20, 85, 145, 168, 192
Arthritis, Old Man, 70
artichokes, 33, 47, 48
Asian vegetables, 17, 18, 31, 34, 115. See
    also specific vegetables
asparagus, 14, 42
avocado, 45, 51, 53, 64, 92, 124, 138

Baby Food Juice, 9
"Bacon Bits," 112, 113
Banana Almond Bread, 174–75
Banana Cocoa Sundae, 196
Banana Cream Shake, 53
Banana Nutmeg Sundae with Pineapple and
    Coconut, 196
Banana Pecan Pancakes, 90–91
bananas, 51, 54, 58, 61–63, 65–72, 75–76,
    79, 83, 88–91, 147, 178, 188, 192,
    194, 198, 199, 201, 205–7, 209
barley, 101
Barley Cereal with Apple and Spice, 85
Basic Spelt Crust, 153, 170, 171
Basil Herb Oil, 148, 159
Basil Mayonnaise, 143
bay leaf, 96, 155
Beach Salad, 122–23

bean soups, 98, 99
bean sprouts, 166
beans, 11, 47, 58, 119, 124, 135, 137, 140, 154
    black, 105
    kidney, 142, 154
    vanilla, 210
    white, 98, 99
Beauty, 10
Beauty Shake, 53
bee propolis, 21
beets, 10, 14, 38, 117, 118, 122, 155
Berries and Cream, 54
bifidus, 56
Big Cleanse, The, 10
bilberry, 78
blackberries, 36, 54, 61, 64
Blackberry Nectarine Fruit Salad, 128
blackstrap molasses, 42, 176
blenders, workhorse, 5
blood cleanse, 35
blueberries, 14, 15, 17, 19, 20, 44, 50, 56, 58, 61–63, 67, 69, 78, 108, 127
bok choy, 18
boysenberries, 36
Brain Juice, 11
Brain Power, 11
bread, 114, 116, 142, 152, 156, 174–77. See also croutons; crusts
breakfast foods, 81–93
Breath Freshener Juice, 12
broccoli, 22, 25, 28, 30, 33, 122, 150, 151, 153, 155, 161, 164
brown rice, 86, 87, 128, 157, 166, 192. See also rice
brownies, 190, 192–93
Brussels sprouts, 51, 52
buckwheat, 71
buckwheat sprouts, 44
burdock, 35, 42
Burgers, Lentil, 156

cabbage, 11, 14, 19, 30, 33, 47, 51, 55, 58, 121
Caesar, Insalata, 115
Caesar Dressing, Creamy, 115, 130
Caesar Salad with Thyme Croutons, 114
cake, 90–91, 180–81
cantaloupe, 9, 20, 22, 23, 34, 41, 60, 68, 70, 128
cardamom, 118, 155, 165
carob, 57, 89, 184, 186, 188, 207, 209
Carob Fruit Bars, 194

Carob Power Brownies, 192–93
Carrot, Pineapple, and Strawberry Juice, 13
Carrot and Soymilk Juice, 12
Carrot Sunflower Granola, 84
Carrot Walnut Cake, 180–81
carrots, 9, 10, 21, 38, 40, 42, 45, 47, 48, 67, 74, 90, 96–98, 100, 104, 114, 116, 120–23, 126, 139, 150, 154–56, 165, 186, 194, 201
cashew butter, 69, 156
cashews, 123, 124, 156, 164, 173
cauliflower, 10, 25, 51, 98, 155, 164
cayenne peppers, 35, 50, 64, 79, 144
celery, 12, 21, 25–27, 31, 33–35, 38, 40, 44, 47, 49, 58, 72, 74, 96–98, 101, 107, 111, 116, 120, 125, 126, 142, 155
Celery Lane, 13
Celery Potato Soup, 102
celery salt, 92
celery seeds, 102, 120
centrifugal juicers, 5, 6
cereal, 85, 86
    grain flake, 195
chamomile, 40
chard, 10, 23, 64, 117
cheese, soy, 103, 114, 116, 150–53, 162
Chef's Salad, A, 112–13
cherries, 17, 47, 60, 82, 108
Cherry Fruit Pops, 202
Cherry Grape Kanten, 208–9
Cherry Peach Velvet, 54–55
Cherry Yogurt Sauce, 210
chickpeas. See garbanzo beans
chili peppers, 74, 92, 134, 154, 160, 161
chili powder, 142, 160
Chilled Cucumber Mint Soup, 107
chlorophyll, 45
Chlorophyll Ya Up, 14
Chocolate Coconut Pops, 199
Cholesterol Reducer, 55
Chutney, Cranberry, 146
Cilantro Mint Dressing, 134–35
Cilantro Pesto Sauce, 136–37, 152
Cinnamon Fruit Soup, 109
Classic Vegetable Stock, 96, 97
Clean Colon, 56
cleanses/cleansing, 10. See also detoxification
    blood, 35
    colon, 56, 59
    gall, 33
    head, 26
    liver, 33
cloves, 180

Cobbler, Apple Pecan, 168–69
Cocktail, Super VJ, 74–75
Cocoa Coconut Frosting, 176, 177
Cocoa Kasha with Bananas, 89
coconut, 88, 173, 177, 184, 188, 194, 196, 198, 199, 201, 205
coconut milk, 42, 54, 57, 78, 210
coenzyme Q_{10} (CoQ_{10}), 27
coffee substitute, grain, 74
Cold Cherry Soup, 108–9
Coleslaw with Fresh Dill, 121
collard greens, 10, 11, 14, 22, 43, 64
Color Purple, The, 14
cookies, 182–87
Cool Breeze, 57
coolers, 15, 28–29, 32, 68–69, 73
coriander, 156, 160
corn, 124, 154
cornmeal, 173
cranberry, 52, 54, 59, 63, 64, 78
Cranberry Chutney, 146
Cranberry Cooler, 15
Cream of Rice with Peaches and Honey, 87
Creamsicle Pops, 198–99
Creamy Caesar Dressing, 115, 130
Creamy Italian Dressing, 112, 130–31
Creamy Tomato Soup, 103
Crispies Treats, Grain, 195
croutons, 112, 114–16
crusts, 153, 170–73, 181
cucumber, 10, 12, 20, 21, 26, 31, 34, 35, 42, 47, 49–51, 53, 98, 107, 124
Cucumber, Lime, and Kiwi Divine, 16
Cucumber Coolade, 16
Cucumber Raita Salad, 118–19
cumin, 92, 142, 144
currants, black, 61
Curried Orange Sauce, 137
Curried Red Lentil Stew, 155
Curried Waldorf Salad, 112
Curry Mayonnaise, 112, 144
custard, 181

dandelion flowers and stems, 41
dandelion greens, 28
dandelion leaves, 63
dandelion roots, 35, 63
Date Fudge Brownies, 190
Date Nut Crust, 172–73
Date Supreme, 57
dates, 67, 87, 88, 145, 168, 176, 178, 180, 182, 184, 186, 188, 195, 201, 208
Deep Sea Juicing, 17

Deep Sleeper, 58
Delicious Detox, 17
desserts, 167–211
Detox Tonic, 18
detoxification, 17, 38, 46, 49, 59. See also cleanses
dietary approach to change, 3
dieting, 214–15
Dijon Salad Dressing, 114, 117, 131
dill, 101–3, 119–21
Dill Mayonnaise, 119, 144
dips, 138–41, 153
diuretics, 46
Dream Shake, 58
dressings, 130–35
dulse, 17, 31

Eastern Wonder, 18
eating habits, 214–15
echinacea, 63
egg substitute, vegetarian, 90, 170, 172, 174, 176, 178, 180, 184, 186, 190, 194
eggplant, 154
endive, 30, 117, 122
energizers, 21, 61, 76
Enzyme Enhancer, 19
escarole, 98
Everglades Punch, 19
exercise, 213
Eye Essentials, 20

"Fakin' Bacon," 92
farina, 87
Fast-Astic Juice, 20
fasting, 20
Fatigue Buster, 21
fats, 215
fennel bulb, 122
fennel flowers and stems, 79
Fettucine with Pesto Tomatoes, 150
fish, 116–17, 157–59
Flavorburst, 21
Flax Cruncher, 59
flaxseed meal, 188
flaxseed oil, 41, 78
flaxseeds, 56, 59, 74
flu, 51
food(s)
    focusing on, 215
    healthy vs. junk, 215
    nutrition in outer layers of, 6
    punishing oneself with, 214

Fountain of Youth, 22
Free Radical Delight, 22
Friendly Fiber Colon Cleanse: The Ultimate
    Detox Drink, 59
Frosting, Cocoa Coconut, 176, 177
fructo oligo saccharides, 51
Fruit and Nut Cookies, 186–87
Fruit Bars, Carob, 194
fruit pops, 202
fruit powder, 60
fruit salads, 112, 122, 127, 128, 133
fruit soup, 108–10
Fruity Kazootie, 60
Fruity Party Punch, 60

gall flush, 33
garbanzo beans, 135, 137, 140, 154
Gary Null's Muscle-Building Shake, 61
Gary's Gingerale, 23
Gary's "Wake Up" Shake, 61
Gazpacho, Some're Cool, 106
Gimme a Juice with Everything, 23
gingerale, 8, 23
Gingerbread, 176–77
Gingermint Tea, 24
Gingery Bean Soup, 99
Gingery Carrot Soup, 100
Ginkgo biloba, 11
ginseng, 11, 21, 61
go chi berries, 18
goal-setting (weight loss), 214
Grain Crispies Treats, 195
granola, 57, 84
Granola Delight, 207
grapefruit, 18, 19, 21, 39, 49, 62, 68, 204
grapes, 14, 52, 65, 108, 208
    with seeds, 8, 20, 22, 25, 43, 47
Green Bean Salad with Almonds and Dill,
    119
green beans, 11, 47, 58
Green Pepper Apple Juice, 24
green peppers, 96, 136, 154. See also peppers
Green Power Punch, 25
green tea, 15, 31
green vegetable powder, 31, 62, 188
Greens and Grapes, 25
Groovy Ruby, 62
Guacamole and Bermuda Onion Dip,
    138–39, 153
guarana, 21
guava, 33, 45
Guava-Cucumber Juice, 26

Halibut with Tomato Salsa, 157
Hannah's Smoothie, 62
Head Cleaner, 26
Healthy Fondue, 209
Healthy Munchie Shake, 63
Healthy Smile, 27
Heart, Sweet, 47
Hearty Oats with Nuts and Raisins, 83
Heavenly Roasted Nuts, 90, 122
Holiday Surprise Cookies, 184–85
Honey Honey Dandelion, 28
Honey Peanut Topping, 188
honeydew, 8, 19, 28, 198, 200, 203
Honeydew and Yam Juice, 27
Honeymint Cooler, 28–29
huckleberries, 20
Hummus, Lemony, 140
hunger, 214–15

ice cream, nondairy, 67, 68, 197, 207
Immune, 29
Immune Movement, 63
Inner Clear, 64
Inner Heat, 64–65
Insalata Caesar, 115
isolation, social, 214

jalapeño peppers, 105, 138
Japanese Rice with Shiitake Mushrooms,
    166
Joint Power, 30
Ju Ju Juice, 30
Juice from the Ocean, 31
juicers, 5, 6
    for wheatgrass, 10, 14, 40, 44
juices, 8–50
juicing
    basics, 5–6
    benefits, 4

kale, 23, 25, 31, 33, 44, 48, 70, 98
kasha, 89
kava kava, 40
kelp, 34
kidney beans, 142, 154
King of Chlorophyll: The Greenest Juice in
    Town, 31
kiwi, 16, 18, 19, 21, 31, 43, 197
Kiwi Green Cooler, 32
Kiwi Lime Pops, 200
Kiwi Smoothie, 65
kombu, 17, 31

Lasagna, Mushroom, 150–51
lecithin, 27, 41, 58, 62, 92
leechi nuts, 11
leeks, 101, 102, 104, 162
Lemon Garlic Dressing, 124, 132
Lemon Lime Slush, 203
lemons/lemon juice, 15, 18–20, 24, 28,
    34–35, 38, 39, 45, 48, 53, 54, 66, 68,
    90, 106, 108, 111, 116, 121, 123–28,
    130, 132–35, 138, 144, 161, 168, 173,
    181, 198, 200, 202, 208
Lemony Hummus, 140
Lentil Burgers, 156
lentil sprouts, 118, 156
lentils, 155, 156
lettuce, 17, 112, 117, 122
lima beans, 124
limes/lime juice, 15, 16, 18, 19, 28, 31,
    35–37, 39, 47, 48, 52, 54, 65, 68, 70,
    73, 74, 92, 100, 110, 128, 132, 142,
    200, 203, 204
Live Breakfast Porridge, 82
live food, 3
Liver Cleanse, 33
Liver/Gall Flush, 33
Living Protein Squares, 188–89
lotus, Chinese, 18
Lungs, Strong, 45

macadamia butter, 69
macadamia nuts, 168, 194
main dishes, 149–66
Mango Fruit Pops, 202
Mango Lassi, 66
mangoes, 11, 19, 76, 205
Matar Paneer, 160
mayonnaise, 112, 119, 143–44
    soy, 116, 120, 121, 126, 143, 144
Medjool Date Bottom, 188
melon. See also cantaloupe; honeydew;
    watermelon
    oriental, 18
Melon Boost, 34
Midday Refresher, 34
Mighty Berry Smoothie, The, 66
milk, 77. See also soymilk
    coconut, 42, 54, 78, 210
    rice, 57, 59, 66, 67, 74, 75, 207
milk thistle, 33
millet, 71, 88, 97, 116, 124, 142
mint, 28, 31, 107, 109, 134
mint julep leaves, 44, 57

Mint Shake, 67
mint sprigs, 110
miso, brown rice, 104
Mister Clean Blood, 35
mitsuba, Japanese, 18
Mixed Citrus Vinaigrette, 122, 132
Mixed Dark Green Salad, 117
Mixed Sprout Salad, 118
Morning After, The, 35
Most Decadent Health Shake in Town, The,
    67
Muscle Performance, 68
mushroom, 92
    shiitake, 104, 166
Mushroom Barley Soup, 101
Mushroom Broccoli Quiche, 153
Mushroom Lasagna, 150–51
mustard, 92, 121, 131, 144

Naples Cooler, 68–69
Nature's Total Salad, 124
nectarine, 110, 128, 204
nori, sushi, 115
Nuts and Seeds, 69

oat bran, 71, 192
oatmeal, 74
oats, 83, 84, 184, 186
Old Man Arthritis, 70
olives, 29, 42, 112, 124
onions, 26, 29, 64, 92, 96, 98, 100, 106,
    112, 120, 124, 126, 136, 138, 142,
    145, 146, 154–56, 160. See also leeks;
    scallions
Orange Apricot Spread, 145
Orange-Berry Lime Slush, 36
orange peel, 23, 145, 168
oranges/orange juice, 11, 15, 19, 22, 23, 26,
    30, 33, 37, 39, 48, 49, 68, 70, 78, 85,
    108, 109, 132, 133, 168, 180, 197–99,
    204, 211
organic food, 6
Oriental Miso Vegetable Soup, 104

Pancakes, Banana Pecan, 90–91
papaya, 19, 23, 30, 37, 43, 59, 76, 78
Papaya Nectar Soup, 110
Papaya Squash Soup, 108
Papaya the Sailor Man, 36
paprika, 125, 126, 130
Paradise Drink, The, 37
parsley, 132

parsnips, 10, 42, 162, 172, 182, 190, 191, 195
passion fruit, 21, 79
passivity, 213
pasta, whole grain, 122, 124, 150, 151
Pasta and White Bean Soup, 98
PC Smoothie, The, 70
pea pods, snow, 104
peaches, 11, 17, 54, 62, 65, 70, 72, 74, 82, 87, 127, 208
peanut butter, 62, 188, 195
Peanut Butter Honey Spread, 147
pears, 8, 16, 21, 35, 41, 43, 56, 58, 62, 68, 83, 109, 111, 168, 209
peas, 160
Peas Pillau with Cinnamon, 165
Pecan Chewies, 191
pecans, 77, 86, 91, 168, 172, 180, 184, 186, 194, 199
peppermint, 12, 24, 28, 64, 73, 76
peppers
    bell, 24, 74, 92, 96, 106, 107, 118, 122, 125, 136, 154, 164
    cayenne, 35, 50, 64, 79, 144
    chili, 74, 92, 134, 154, 160, 161
    jalapeño, 105, 138
pesto, 136–38, 150, 152, 159
Phyto-Fiber, 71
Pie, Sweet Potato, 170
pine nuts, 122
pineapple, 10, 13, 19, 27, 30, 31, 37, 46, 48, 52, 54, 70, 79, 196, 197, 202, 205, 208
Pineapple Orange Slush, 204
pita bread, 152
Pizza, Zesty Italian, 152
pomegranate seeds, 107, 108
poppy seeds, 119
pops, 198–202
Porridge, Live Breakfast, 82
Potato Aid, 37
potatoes, 50, 56, 75, 102, 120, 162
Pride of the Detox Juices, 38
probiotic, 51
procrastination, 213
Prostate Pro, 38–39
protein powder, 22, 23, 37, 49, 54, 61, 63, 66–68, 72, 76
psyllium/bifidus, 56, 59
Pudding, Tropical Ambrosia, 205
pulp, 6
pumpkin, 55

Pumpkin and Spice Muffins, 178–79
pumpkin seeds, 38
Pure Citrus Punch, 39

quinoa, 82, 124, 173

radish sprouts, 118
radishes, 18, 44
raisins, 83, 84, 86, 91, 111, 123, 178, 184, 186, 205, 206
raspberries, 17, 34, 36, 66, 72, 127, 207, 211
Raspberry Coulis, Red, 181, 211
Raspberry Crowned Lemon Tart, 181–82
Raspberry Melon Pops, 200
red peppers, 33, 107, 118, 125, 164. See also peppers, bell
Red Potato Salad, 120
Red Raspberry Coulis, 181, 211
Relax, 40
Relaxer, 40–41
relish, sweet, 125
rice
    brown, 86, 87, 128, 157, 166, 192
    puffed, 59
    white Basmati, 165
rice bran, 192
rice bread, 116
rice cereal, 87
rice flour, 192
rice frozen dessert, 209
rice milk, 57, 59, 66, 67, 74, 75, 207
rice protein powder, 76. See also protein powder
rice syrup, 128, 191, 195
ripeness of produce, 6
Rock Hard, 41
romaine lettuce, 17, 112, 114, 115, 124
Roots of Wisdom, 42

saffron, 165, 206
salads, 111–28
Salmon with Teriyaki Sauce, 158
sauces, 136–38, 150–52, 158, 159, 181, 206, 210–11
Savory Croutons, 112, 115, 116
scallions, 104, 123, 161, 166
Scalloped Autumn Vegetables, 162–63
sea vegetables/seaweed, 17, 31, 34, 115
seafood, 116–17, 157–59
seeds, 6, 69, 102, 107, 108, 119, 120, 138. See also flaxseed; sunflower seeds
    grapes with, 8, 20, 22, 25, 43, 47

seltzer, 46. *See also* sparkling water

sesame oil, 104, 133, 161, 165. *See also* tahini

Sesame Orange Dressing, 118, 133

shakes, 51–79

shiitake mushroom, 104, 166

Skin Elixir, 42

Sleeper, Deep, 58

slush, 36, 203–5

Smooth Vanilla Sauce, 181, 210–11

Sole with Walnut Pesto Sauce, 159

Some're Cool Gazpacho, 106

soups, 95–110

Southwestern Squash Soup, 105

soy, 68, 197, 207. *See also* tempeh; tofu

soy butter, 69

soy cheese, 103, 114, 116, 150–53, 162

soy mayonnaise, 116, 120, 121, 126, 143, 144

soy protein powder, 76. *See also* protein powder

soy sauce, 92, 123, 126, 130, 134, 158, 161, 166

Soy Wonder, 72

soy yogurt, 51, 59, 63, 64, 177

soymilk, 12, 53, 54, 57, 67, 69, 72, 86, 87, 89, 102, 109, 160, 162, 171, 176, 210

sparkling water, 8, 23, 44, 46, 60, 197

spelt bread, 156

Spelt Crust, Basic, 153, 170, 171

spelt flour, 174, 176, 178, 180, 182, 184, 186, 190, 194

Spice of Life, The, 43

Spicy Texas Chili, 154

spinach, 11, 14, 20, 22, 23, 25, 27, 31, 33, 35, 36, 38, 43, 64

spreads, 142–48

Spritzer, Summertime, 46

Sprout Power, 44

squash, 99, 103–5, 108, 109, 124, 154. *See also* zucchini

acorn, 162

St. John's wort, 40

Stamina, 72–73

Stir-Fried Broccoli with Tempeh and Lemon Threads, 161–62

Stomach Settler, 44–45

strawberries, 13, 19, 23, 30, 36, 40, 51, 54, 60, 62, 63, 66, 68, 108, 127

Strawberry Chocolate Pops, 198

Strawberry Compote with Saffron Flowers, 206–7

Strawberry Mint Cooler, 73

Strong Lungs, 45

"Sublime" Water Slush, The, 204–5

Succotash Salad, 124–25

Summer Fruit Salad, 127

Summertime Spritzer, 46

sundaes, 196

sunflower butter, 69

Sunflower Salad Dressing, 134

sunflower seeds, 84, 92, 116, 124, 126, 184, 188, 192

sunflower sprouts, 44

Sunny Day Crust, A, 173, 181

Sunrise Oatmeal Shake, 74

Super VJ Cocktail, 74–75

sushi nori, 115

Sweet and Sour Watermelon Juice, 46

Sweet Heart, 47

Sweet Kidney Bean Mash, 142–43

Sweet Potato Crust, 172

Sweet Potato Pie, 170

Sweet Potato Shake, 75

sweet potatoes, 139, 142, 178, 180, 184

Sweet Rice Cream Cereal, 86

Swordfish with Basil Herb Oil, 159

Tabouli Salad, 123

tahini, 130, 140

Tahini Garbanzo Bean Dressing, 135, 164

tangerines, 21, 29, 197, 205

Tangy Carrot Dip, 139

Tea Shake, 76

tempeh, 92, 93, 161

Tempeh "Turkey" Salad, 126–27

teriyaki sauce, 158

Tex-Mex Tofu Scrambler, 92–93

Thyme Croutons, 114

tofu, 59, 72, 92, 104, 113, 124, 130, 134, 138, 139, 153, 160, 205, 208

Tomato Garlic Pasta Salad, 122

Tomato Salad Dressing, 133

Tomato Salsa, 122, 141, 157

tomatoes, 22, 34, 50, 72, 74, 92, 98, 99, 103, 105, 106, 118, 136, 138, 150, 152–55, 160, 161

sun-dried, 152

Trip to Brussels, A, 51

Tropical Ambrosia Pudding, 205

Tropical Millet Delight, 88

Tropical Pops, 201

tuna, 116

"Turkey" Salad, Tempeh, 126–27

turmeric, 92, 144, 160

turnips, 26

Ultra Marathon Energy Shake, 76

valerian, 40, 58
vanilla bean, 210
Vegetable Millet Soup, 97
Veins Be Gone, 47
Velvety Pecan Milk, 77
Very Jerry Berry, 78
vinegar, 92, 158
    apple cider, 121, 131, 139, 145, 160, 161
Vision, 78
vitamin C, 34, 60, 66

wakame, 17, 31
Waldorf Salad, Curried, 112
walnut butter, 136, 138
Walnut Pesto Sauce, 138, 150, 159
walnuts, 70, 83, 90, 111, 117, 178, 180,
    184, 190
water, sparkling, 8, 23, 44, 46, 60
watermelon, 17, 18, 20, 34, 43, 46, 48, 200,
    204
Watermelonade, 48
Weight Loss Juice, 48
weight-loss tips, 213–15
Weight Reducer, 49

Well-Being, 79
wheat, bulgar, 123
wheat bread, 152
wheat flour, 91
wheat germ, 91
wheatgrass juice, 6, 10, 14, 40, 44
whole food, 6
wine, red, 8
Wonder Juice Float, 197

Yam Juice, 49
yams, 9, 20, 27, 70–72, 142
yogurt, 107
    nondairy, 51, 59, 63, 64, 72, 100, 103,
        105, 106, 110, 118, 177, 198, 199,
        210
yohimbe, 41
You Say Tomato, I Say Potato, 50
Yummy, 50

Zesty Cauliflower with Garlic and Tahini,
    164
Zesty Italian Pizza, 152
Zesty Tomato Sauce, 136, 151
Zesty Tuna Salad, 116–17
zucchini, 22, 43, 92, 97, 101, 154, 166